Sven Lindqvist was born in 1932 in Stockholm, where he still lives. Since 1955 he has published more than thirty books of essays, aphorisms, autobiography, documentary prose, travel and literary reportage. He is the author of *Bench Press*, an autobiographical essay on gym culture, which ends with him leaving for the Sahara. His intellectual adventures in the desert are followed up in the highly acclaimed *Desert Divers* and *'Exterminate all the Brutes'*, a journey to the roots of European racism via the study of a sentence in Joseph Conrad's *Heart of Darkness*. He is also the author of *A History of Bombing*, also published by Granta.

Sarah Death has translated Sven Lindqvist's *Bench Press* and works by various other Swedish authors. She was awarded the George Bernard Shaw Prize for translation from Swedish in 2003 and 2006.

Terra Nullius

A Journey Through No One's Land

SVEN LINDQVIST

Translated by Sarah Death

Granta Books

London

Granta Publications, 12 Addison Avenue, London W11 4QR

First published in Great Britain by Granta Books 2007
Published by arrangement with The New Press, New York
This edition published by Granta Books 2008
First published in Sweden under the title *Terra nullius:*
En resa genom ingens land by Albert Bonniers Förlag, 2005

A CIP catalogue record for this book
is available from the British Library.

1 3 5 7 9 10 8 6 4 2

ISBN 978 1 864708 005 9

Printed and bound in Great Britain
by William Clowes Ltd, Beccles, Suffolk

Contents

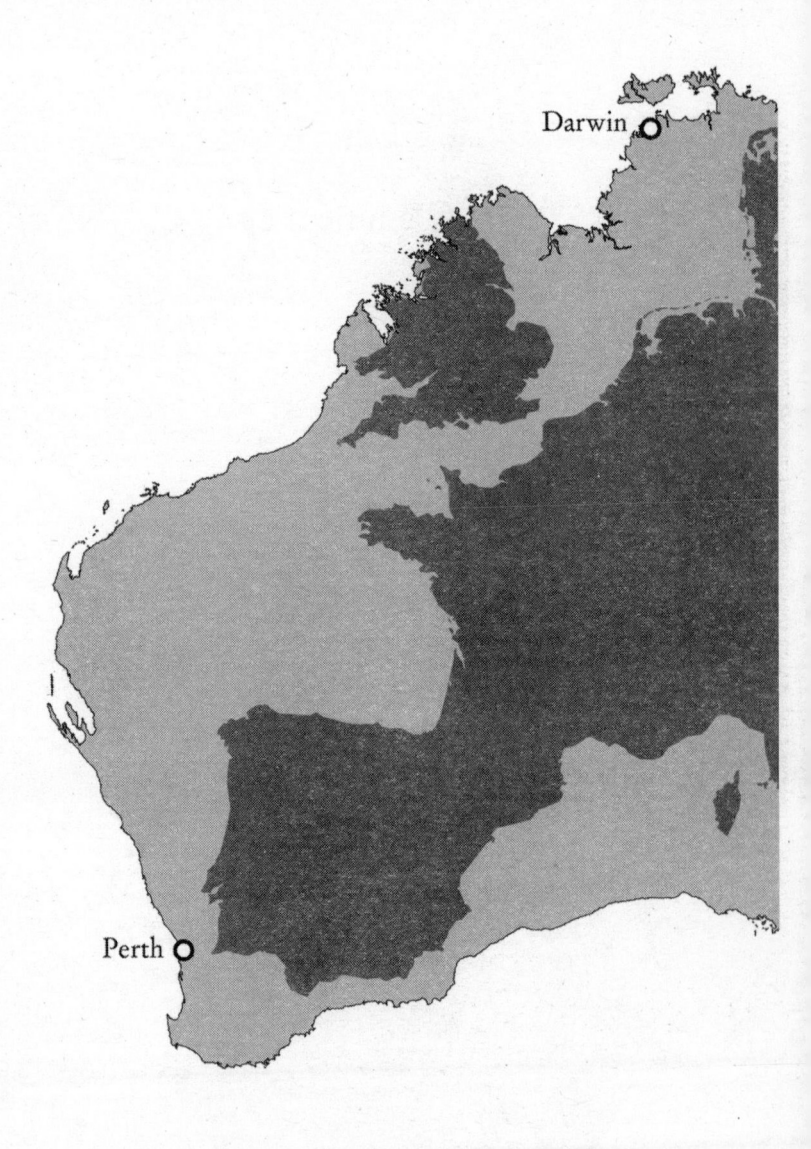

Map of Europe enclosed in that of Australia.

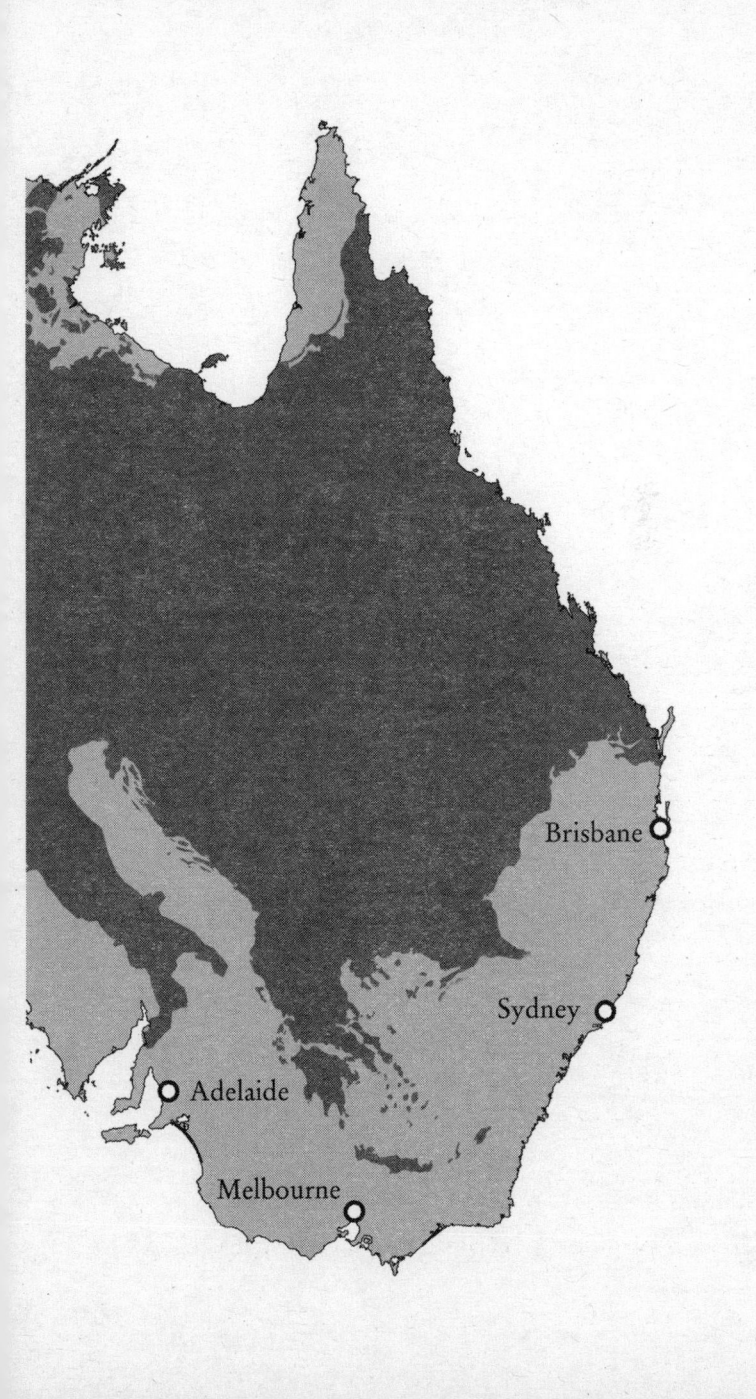

Brisbane

Sydney

Adelaide

Melbourne

Terra Nullius

To Moorundie

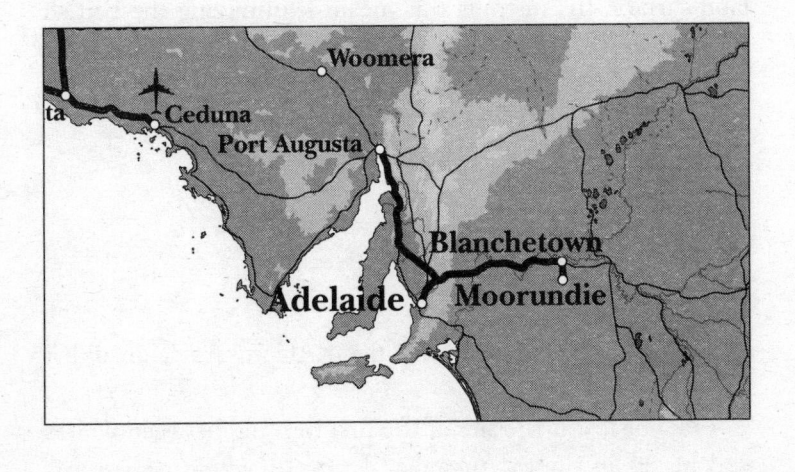

1

Terra nullius. From the Latin *terra*, earth, ground, land, and *nullius*, no one's.

Thus: no one's land, land not belonging to anybody. Or at any rate, not to anybody that counts.

Originally: land not belonging to the Roman Empire.

In the Middle Ages: land not belonging to any Christian ruler.

Later: land to which no European state as yet lays claim. Land that justly falls to the first European state to invade the territory.

Empty land. Uninhabited land. Land that will soon be uninhabited because it is populated by inferior races, condemned by the laws of nature to die out. Land where the original inhabitants are, or can soon be rendered, so few in number as to be negligible.

The legal fictions summed up as *terra nullius* were used to justify the European occupation of large parts of the global land surface. In Australia this meant legitimizing the British invasion and its accompanying acts of dispossession and the destruction of indigenous society.[1]

2

Moorundie? Morrundie? No, the RAC in Adelaide didn't know anything about it.

'Oh, but it was the site of the first fighting between whites and blacks in South Australia,' I said. 'A whole people was wiped out, the Ngaiawong people.[2] There must at least be a memorial or something.'

No, the name wasn't on any of their maps or itineraries. They sent me to the South Australian Museum, which didn't know anything about Moorundie either. The indigenous population live in the museum's exhibition in a continuous now, in an eternally timeless, permanent present that has neither a future nor a history. On the subject of what the white invasion did to those who were invaded, the museum is silent.

'Oh, but it was where the explorer Edward John Eyre began his scientific investigation of the Aboriginal peoples of Australia. It was in Moorundie he collected the material for his treatise "Manners and Customs of the Aborigines of Australia",[3] which is the gateway to everything this museum has on show about them . . .'

No, the museum's information desk apologized and referred me to the tourist office, which sent me on to another tourist office, which didn't know anything either. Moorundie seemed to have been swallowed up by the ground.

3

All around me in Adelaide, Sorry Day was in full swing. 'Sorry' said the placards. 'Sorry' said fifty thousand white demonstrators. They were protesting against their government's refusal to apologize for the injustice that had been done, and was still being done, to Australia's Aborigines. Fifty thousand whites were showing their solidarity with the Aborigines by demanding that their government apologize.

Some of the 950,000 Adelaidians who didn't go on the demonstration took up the gauntlet and answered in the days that followed via the web and the letters columns in the papers. 'Sorry' wasn't just a polite phrase, they pointed out. If the government apologized to the indigenous peoples, the present generation would thereby be accepting responsibility for the crimes of previous generations, for which the time limit for prosecution had long since expired. If the government as much as whispered 'Sorry,' the sluice gates would open and in would pour compensation claims from people who had nothing in common with the victims of those past crimes but the colour of their skin.

'Apologize for what?' asked others. In the conflict there had most definitely been outrages committed on both sides. It was only natural that the technically and militarily more advanced civilization had beaten the technically inferior one. What happened in Australia had also happened in North and South America, in Siberia and Central Asia. Large areas of the globe are today populated by European immigrants who have ousted the original population. Who often in their turn have ousted even earlier inhabitants. Should they all be paid compensation? And in that case, who's to pay? For what?

4

I finally located Moorundie/Morrundie on a computer in the map section of the Department of the Environment. It turned out to be on the Murray River just south of Blanchetown.

One chilly, brilliant June morning, I drive out of Adelaide. The vineyards are turning green, the wheat is glistening in rust-brown fields, the bluebushes of the heathlands are strewn with stars. The occasional gravelled road, bright white like those on the Swedish island of Gotland, tells of underlying limestone. The occasional long, treeless hill lends a Scottish air.

In this landscape we find neither neither spruce nor pine, neither birch nor lime, neither oak nor elm. Here we have acacia and eucalyptus, full stop. But in Australia, these two species seem able to assume whatever form they like. Since there are only two trees here, those two have arrayed themselves in all the rich variety of forms that on other continents are divided between many different species and families.

The crowns of the trees float like clouds in the sky. The foliage appears to hover in the air, resting lazily on nothingness. Suddenly, something that looks like the crown of a dill plant is sticking up above the other treetops. Just as suddenly, the landscape presents me with a bouquet of trees held together by the damp fist of a rootball half buried in the ground.

Below Blanchetown, the river is sluggish and silty. It creates a lush, damp environment in the riverbed. A little gravel track runs by the waterside. The name 'Moorundie' is associated above all with an island in the river, created by the silt.

5

John Eyre came here on 15 June 1839, and thought he'd found paradise. Here was every possible requirement for the good life: running water, tall trees, fertile soil and thousands of birds and fish, in fact the ideal site for a settlement. He hurried back to Adelaide and bought 1,411 acres of land at Moorundie from the government of the newly founded colony. Now he was a landowner in paradise.[4]

An unspoken condition of the sale was that the land did not belong to anyone else; that it was what was called 'terra nullius', no one's land.

There was just one catch: Moorundie wasn't uninhabited. The Ngaiawong people had been living there for at least five thousand years and had every intention of staying. Every time a herd of cattle was driven across the continent from the old penal colonies of Sydney and Melbourne in the east to the new settler colony of Adelaide, there was conflict when they reached Moorundie. A contemporary commentator summed up the situation: 'Whenever the parties of whites happened to be of sufficient force, a great slaughter was sure to be committed upon the blacks.'

Eyre noted in his diary: 'But the only idea of the men was retaliation – to shoot every native they saw.' Such shotgun progress may have eased their passage on that one occasion, but it created problems for the cattle herds to follow and for the whites who wanted to settle in the valley.

As predicted, the conflict intensified from year to year, culminating in 1841 in a massacre in which white troops mowed down a large group of Aborigines, regardless of their age or sex. The officially recorded death toll was thirty. According to the Aborigines the real figure was much higher.[5]

After the massacre, Eyre was appointed District Chief in Moorundie, with the task of getting to know the natives and resolving the conflict. On leaving his post three years later, he could boast there had not been a single instance in that period of Europeans suffering serious injury or being attacked by the indigenous people. Eyre also succeeded in preventing the whites' worst abuses of power. He introduced a paternalist regime with a monthly distribution of flour and sugar. But he could do nothing to stop Aboriginal society disintegrating. The black people succumbed to white diseases, and the cramped conditions in the camps where they received their rations encouraged the rapid spread of infection. White men without women chased after black women and passed on sexually transmitted diseases. In 1841 these were still unknown in Moorundie; three years later, many were dying from them.

A few decades later, an entire people had vanished. No one

spoke their language any more. No one preserved their holy places. There is not so much as a memorial left.

Was it genocide? If so, when did it become genocide? When they shot every Aborigine they saw? When they bought or raped the women and infected them with syphilis? Or even further back, when they took land at gunpoint and bought peace with rations of flour?

'Genocide was a concept that didn't yet exist,' say those who don't want to apologize. It took another hundred years for the word 'genocide' to come into use, and even longer for it to assume any legal force. It is anachronistic to judge the people of the 1840s by the laws and morals of our time. They couldn't know that what they were doing would at some future date be considered wrong. Genocide presumes intent. But those settlers in Moorundie didn't foresee the consequences of their actions. They didn't realize the natives would die out. They can't be guilty of something they were unable to predict.

But the truth is, the fate of the Aborigines could be all too clearly predicted. In 1837 a British parliamentary committee looked at the situation of the indigenous peoples of the whole empire, from Newfoundland, where the last native was shot dead in 1823, to South Africa and Australia, where whole peoples were *en route* to extinction. The committee found that the Europeans had unlawfully conquered the natives' territory, decimated their numbers and undermined their way of life. 'Injustice and cruelty' were the main causes of the extinction of the indigenous peoples.[6]

After three years in Moorundie, Eyre reached the same conclusion.

It is an undeniable fact, that wherever European colonies have been established in Australia, the native races in that neighbourhood are rapidly decreasing, and already in some of the elder settlements, have totally disappeared. It is equally indisputable that the presence of the white man has been the sole agent in producing so lamentable an effect; that the . . . result must be that if nothing be done to check it, the whole of the Aboriginal tribes of Australia will be swept away from the face of the earth.

To sanction this aggression we have not, in the abstract, the slightest shadow of either right or justice – we have not even the extenuation of endeavouring to compensate those we have injured, or the merit of attempting to mitigate the sufferings our presence inflicts.[7]

And that's why the calls are still echoing today round the buildings in Adelaide: Say sorry! Give redress! Make amends for the sins of the past!

7

As a very young man, I went to Iceland aboard a ship that stopped off in the Trondheimfjord in Norway to load herring barrels.

It was the summer of 1951, a lovely evening at hay-making time. The smell of freshly cut hay was heady and intense. The captain stayed aboard but the first mate and the Icelandic crew rowed ashore. They let me come along. The Icelanders had been there many times before and were welcome guests, invited in for coffee at farmstead after farmstead. There was much chatting and laughing and the mood was high-spirited – until someone caught sight of me sitting over by the door with a sugar lump between my teeth, drinking my coffee from my saucer as the custom was in those days.

'Who's that?'

'He's a passenger,' the Icelanders replied. 'Swedish.'

'Swedish!' The whole room fell silent. All conversation stopped, every smile faded. They all looked at me. The silence seemed interminable. At last the great-grandmother said:

'Swedish, eh? Well what about the 1942 transits, then?'

What could I say? The transport of German troops through Sweden to Norway and back had in fact gone on for several years. But that was how she put it – 'Well what about the 1942 transits, then?' And everybody was waiting for an answer. I tried to make light of it:

'I was ten in 1942. They didn't ask me.'

'But big enough to share the booty,' said the great-grand-mother.

The silence became unbearable. I said thank you for the coffee and crept out with my tail between my legs. I thought it so utterly unfair. Why accuse little me for what the whole Swedish nation had done or not done? As if it was my fault. As if it was my responsibility.

I climbed down the steep edge of the fjord. It was a light evening, the scents were overpowering. The rowing boat we'd come in had dropped several metres with the outgoing tide. While I waited for the others, I silently composed a grand speech in my defence. 'It's wrong to burden children with blame for their parents' actions. Every new generation is born free of guilt.'

But of course that wasn't strictly true. The national debt is passed on from generation to generation. Just like the nation's assets, which amount to a great deal more than its debt. Simply by being born Swedish, I was born rich. It wasn't my own efforts that had made me better off than a Congolese or an Indonesian. It was as the heir to an undamaged society and a fully functioning economy; in short, it was as a Swede that I was well off.

And having accepted the advantages of being a Swede, how could I then disown the disadvantages? The ore consignments, the traffic of soldiers going on leave and other gross breaches of neutrality were what enabled Sweden to keep on good terms with the Germans and avoid the war. It was my own country's cowardly appeasement policy I had to thank for never having been bombed or shot at or even having to go to bed hungry. Yes, the great-grandmother was right. I'd had my share of the booty, so I had to take my share of the responsibility, too.

The Secret of the Desert

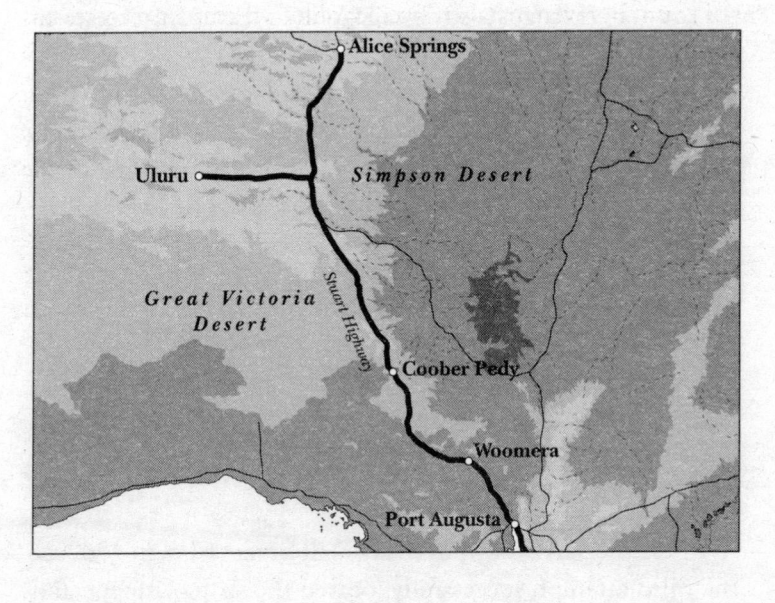

8

Swann Reach Hotel, not far from Moorundie, is shockingly overpriced for what it has to offer. The hollow, sagging beds seem designed for dromedaries. After a bitterly cold night, spent fully dressed under a double layer of covers, I fumble my way through the self-service breakfast. The morning mist over the river and the ferry berth are pewter grey, just like the heath.

Then the sun rises; at a stroke the whole scene is trans-formed. Suddenly you can *see* it all: Charon in his little car ferry across the river, the indecently naked trunks of the euca-lyptus trees, the slender pepper tree beneath which the car is parked.

I continue north via Gladstone, through a Mediterranean landscape that gives way to waterlogged saltmarsh down by the coast. Port Augusta sits by a lagoon in the inner recesses of the bay.

I spend the night at the Pastoral Hotel. The reception desk is in the gaming hall, which is an electronic hell of flashing, bleeping slot machines. An Aboriginal woman is standing there changing her money into counters. She plays 'The Desert Is in Flower' and 'Lucky Clover', she plays 'Blue Lagoon' and 'Dingo Night'. Outside in the street her daughter, who looks about six, sits waiting for her.

She's the first Aborigine I've seen on my trip. We avoid eye contact.

The steppe, flat and empty, starts just outside the town. To the west is the Great Victoria Desert, to the east the Simpson Desert.

It was the surveyor John McDouall Stuart who, in 1862, at the third attempt, successfully located the strip of steppe and savannah between the two deserts that makes it possible to cross Australia from coast to coast, south to north. He was applauded, fêted, given a noble title – and died, forgotten, as an alcoholic in London four years later.[8] But the road he discov-ered is still called the Stuart Highway.

A red road through dry, white grass. Nowhere is the horizon more important than in the desert. A sword-cut divides earth and sky. The landscape is vast, the skyscape even vaster.

Some kilometres east of the main highway lies Woomera, a small, symmetrical settlement of bungalows, planned as a single unit and built in 1947. The British needed somewhere to live while they were testing their intercontinental guided missiles. The huge test site extended from the launch pads in Woomera to the Australian west coast at Port Hedland – a stretch of 2,400 kilometres of no-man's-land with just a few farms, or 'stations', as the Australians call them.[9]

White stations, of course. The blacks didn't count.

On six properties, the farmhouses were moved, relocated outside the risk area. Women and children were evacuated. Telephone warnings were given before each launch. Full compensation was promised for any injury.

When tests involving Black Knight missiles began in 1955, £30,000 was spent on building shelters at six farmhouses and eleven outstations. A further £8,000 went on the extension of telephone lines.

The Aborigines had neither stations nor telephones. They were scattered over an area the size of western Europe, no one knew quite where. Most of this territory was 'reserved' for the Aborigines. In the 1930s it had been allocated to them 'in perpetuity'. Yet in the 1940s, the reservation was reappropriated and turned into a missile test site. The natives had been given the use of the then worthless land as some sort of compensation for everything else that had been taken from them. Now the land was suddenly needed and at once became a 'prohibited area'.

The welfare of the natives was entrusted to a police officer, W. B. MacDougall. Stationed in Woomera, he was supposed to ensure the safety of everyone within an area of over a million square kilometres.

In practice, the whites' noise and refuse proved more dangerous than their missiles. Along the roadsides and around the observation points in the test site accumulated small mountains of the wealthy world's rubbish, to which the Aborigines were drawn once the traffic had frightened off the game they hunted. The nomads of the desert took up residence as scavenging seagulls on the white refuse tips.

10

The abandoned missile launch town survives today as an internment camp for asylum seekers.

Asia has some of the world's most densely populated areas; Australia is the most sparsely populated continent. In fact, when viewed though Chinese or Indonesian eyes, Australia seems virtually unpopulated. The *terra nullius* doctrine used by the British when they occupied Australia would give Asians the right to take over the country.

But white Australians were determined to make the country white. One of the first laws introduced by the Australian Federation was the Immigration Restriction Act of 1901.

The part of it that proved particularly effective for the prevention of non-European immigration was the dictation test. The clause made no mention of race or religion but merely designated unsuitable anyone who could not take down an official fifty words of dictation in a European language. Faced with someone they wanted to let in, they allowed the applicant to choose the language. But they could exclude an Asian applicant with excellent skills in English, German or French quite simply by giving the dictation in some other European language, such as Hungarian.[10]

The dictation test was in use until 1958. Then the Migration Act came into force, making provision for any foreigner without a visa to be interned while his or her case was under consideration. Here again there was no mention of race or religion; in practice, however, the law was not applied to the fifty thousand or so whites staying illegally in Australia – some of them for decades – but only to boat people, refugees from Asia.

They came in the period 1989–94 from Vietnam and Cambodia, in 1994–7 from China, and after 1997 from Iraq and Afghanistan. The total number between 1989 and 1997 was fewer than 3,000, of whom 2,300 were refused entry after their internment.

The internees were considered not to have entered Australia despite their physical presence there; they were classed as 'non-entrants', and detained in six camps in remote parts of the country, Woomera among them.

The first prisoners came here in November 1999. After over a year in detention and with their cases still unresolved, two hundred or, as some say, five hundred refugees broke out of the camp and disappeared. The authorities responded with barbed wire, water cannon, armed guards and a ban on visitors. The internment camps became concentration camps.[11]

Men, women and children stay shut up there for many years, kept in ignorance of their legal rights, deprived of contact with the world around them, in uncertainty, degradation and desperation. The intention is to make internment so unpleasant that it will deter further refugees from seeking asylum in Australia.

'Australian detention practices involve a breach of international, civil, political and human rights,' says Human Rights Commissioner Christopher Sidoti. 'No other western country permits incommunicado detention of asylum seekers.'[12]

In January 2002, it was briefly reported in the world press that Afghan detainees at Woomera had sewn up their mouths to protest against their isolation. Outside the barbed wire there were protests, staged by and large by the same people who are demanding that the government apologize to the Aborigines.

11

According to my Religious Education teacher at secondary school, 'contrition' is at the core of all religions. It's easy to make mistakes. Anybody can make mistakes, even commit crimes. The important thing is knowing how to feel contrition afterwards. That was why he began every lesson with the same question: 'What constitutes contrition?' To this day, I can still rattle off the answer in my sleep:

I realize I have done wrong.

I regret what I have done.

I promise never to do it again.

Today I tend to think these three criteria for contrition are far too introverted. 'Realize', 'regret' and 'promise' can all be done internally, in complete secrecy, without betraying any outward sign of realization or promise. Such an internal contrition process is precious little comfort to the victim of the wrong I committed. And the promise is easily forgotten if nobody knows it was made. So the criteria should demand a more public process of contrition. Perhaps like this:

I freely admit that I have done wrong.

I ask forgiveness of those I have wronged.

I promise to do my best to make amends to them.

Here, the third criterion promises not only that I will not repeat the crime, but also that I will make efforts to put things right to the best of my ability. For the victims, redress is the most tangible result of my contrition and a measure of its sincerity.

Can we feel contrition for other people's crimes? Can we feel contrition for crimes we have not committed personally, but have subsequently profited from? How can we formulate the criteria for contrition to make them applicable to collective responsibility for historical crimes? Perhaps like this:

We freely admit that our predecessors have done wrong and that we are profiting from it.

We ask forgiveness of those who were wronged and of their descendants.

We promise to do our best to make amends to those who were wronged for the effects that still remain.

The larger the collective, the more diluted the personal responsibility. The less intimate the contrition, the greater the risk that it will just be hollow ceremony. A representative steps forward on our behalf, admits the wrong committed, apologizes, pays what it takes and appoints a committee to 'monitor our practices'. Australia isn't even doing that.

Opal is a precious stone that was formed 30 million years ago where deep weathering had caused cracks and voids in porous claystone. In these cavities, the silica in the groundwater was able to accumulate, form a concentrated jelly and crystallize into grape-like, faintly gleaming opals. Australia is the world's greatest producer, and 70 per cent of its production comes from Coober Pedy and adjoining fields along the Stuart Highway 350 kilometres north of Port Augusta.[13]

Rising above the mining fields are the red mesa mountains, 'table mountains' raised above the 'floor' of the surrounding plain and protected by a hard, ferriferous, silica impregnated 'table top'. The landscape is perforated by the underground tunnels of the opal seekers. Holes everywhere – a quarter of a million holes. Everywhere there are spoil-heaps and warnings not to walk on the undermined surfaces.

The first opal was found in 1915 by a fourteen-year-old boy. In 1919, the demobilized soldiers returned from the First World War, experienced in digging trenches. By 1940 the deposits were considered mined out, and there were just a few pensioners left in Coober Pedy. But in 1956 mining operations were mechanized and the town burst back to life – a school in 1961, a small hospital in the same year, a larger, fully equipped one in 1982.

Coober Pedy today is a dusty, run-down gambling den of a town, ruined by alcohol. It is inhabited by three thousand fortune hunters from forty countries, who endure the summer heat and the winter cold by digging themselves into a modern version of catacombs.

They lived originally in abandoned mining tunnels or 'dugouts', dwellings half buried in the hillside, earth cellars, which maintained a more stable inside temperature than walls of thin boarding could provide and were cheaper than proper timber houses. In Coober Pedy today, you can stay in an underground hotel, go to confession in an underground church, shop in an underground bookstore and surf the web from underground internet cafés.

But the smell on the town's breath comes from its bars and liquor stores. 'It's no secret that many in our town have a weakness for alcohol that is slowly destroying both them and the town,' writes the *Coober Pedy Times*. A team of five, appointed to consider appropriate measures, has put forward the following suggestions:

- Daycare provision for alcoholics, offering basic food, showers, laundry, healthcare and activities.
- Alcohol-free premises where people can meet and socialize, free from temptation.
- Licensing restrictions for bars and liquor stores to make alcohol less readily available.
- A mobile patrol to identify and look after alcoholics who have been on a heavy drinking bout, until they sober up.

'Infringement of civil liberties,' say those who make their money out of liquor or are dependent on it. So everything stays the way it is. In Coober Pedy, the very groundwater seems to consist of alcohol. The whole town smells of stale booze.

Fresh rain falls during the night, setting the desert ablaze with flowers, yellow, red and blue. The plain turns green between meres and pools of red water and assumes an almost park-like appearance.

Plants and animals alike live in perpetual expectation of these rare and happy interludes and have developed various strategies for preserving their potential through the dry seasons and making instant use of them when the rains come.

The saltbush is particularly cunning. It has two sorts of seed, the soft and the hard. Termites and other insects prefer to eat the tasty and more accessible soft seeds. This leaves the hard seeds. The soft seeds are more inclined to take risks and will take the chance to grow at the first sign of any moisture. The hard seeds, on the other hand, are preserved in seed-pods and seed-coats containing so much salt that the seed cannot grow until the pod has soaked sufficiently long in a sufficient amount of water for the salt to leach out.

So the hard seed remains sleeping in its salt until large amounts of rain have fallen. Then it grows and the plant quickly develops a deep root system that will allow it to survive even after the surface water that dissolved the salt has dried up.

Large mammals like the red kangaroo are equally well adapted to sudden changes in water supply. After rain, the female will give birth to her young in rapid succession. She will have one joey beside her on the ground, another in her pouch and a third in the form of a fertilized egg inside her body. Each time a new baby is born, the previous one has to vacate the pouch, but it will continue to be suckled by its mother for four months.

The female will now have milk in one teat appropriate for the newborn in her pouch, and in another a different sort of milk suitable for the more mature joey. By producing two different kinds of milk, the kangaroo can make optimum use of the good times for rapid breeding. When drought conditions return, by contrast, fertilization is delayed and the juvenile's development towards sexual maturity slows. Some years later, new rains will trigger a fresh hormone storm and a new set of pregnancies, one after another.[14]

14

For the young, life is from the very outset a matter of extreme helplessness and dependence.

A kangaroo baby is born deaf, blind and no bigger than a little finger. The mother leans back so the baby can crawl up her belly into the pouch and latch on to a teat. The teat engorges to fill the baby's mouth, the edges of which simultaneously tighten so the baby is hanging from the teat. The baby is unable to suckle, so the female injects the milk into its mouth using a special muscle located directly above her mammary glands. She and the baby are so firmly attached that both will bleed if any attempt is made to separate them.

The people of the desert think human beings were originally just as imperfect as baby kangaroos. The Luritja people believe the first people were joined to each other. Their eyes and ears were not open and their arms were still attached along the sides of their torsos. Their legs were pulled up against their bodies. In this helpless state they were cared for by small birds called kurbaru, who fed them with little cakes made of grass seeds.

As a boy, I read about the Luritja people in Nathan Söderblom's *Gudstrons Uppkomst* (*The Origin of Faith in God*, 1914). I read it as a storybook and those stories about the original helplessness of mankind are the only ones I still remember.[15]

The Arrernte people, too, believed all humans were originally conjoined. They were rescued by a primeval creature called the Flycatcher, who used his stone knife to carve out individual human beings. He cut eyes, mouths and noses into their faces, opened their eyes and separated their fingers. He showed them how to make fire and decided whom they could marry.

15

The little roadhouses along the Stuart Highway are a combination of country store, petrol station and café. Young people, chilled by the morning air, warm their hands on mugs of coffee. Wrinkled old cowboys, or stockmen as they are known here, sit with their hats on, as is the custom, having a few beers.

During the day I leave the state of South Australia and proceed into the Northern Territory. Here it has yet to rain. The road is flanked by great red boulders, cracking apart and on their way to crumbling to dust.

I stop to take a closer look at a floury white plant that has folded its leaves together to look like bowls. Some strange flying seeds are making their way on spidery legs ten centimetres long. A lettuce-like plant with muscular leaves the same colour as well-

The effects of desert life on humans.
Illustration from *Bulletin* 1903.

hung meat. Thorny little fruits catch on my socks after only a few steps and carry swiftly on down into my shoes. You remove them at the cost of cutting your fingertips.

The main impression is of overpowering desolation. I

wonder how Aboriginal children would react to the Swedish forests. I know how Faeroese children reacted when they found themselves in Norway. In the 1950s on the Faeroe Islands there were some thirty trees all told. Travelling for hours through millions of trees proved too much for the children, who burst into tears. In much the same way, the emptiness of the interior of Australia can be overwhelming for those used to a livelier field of vision.

To me, this emptiness is liberating. The view in an urban street changes from one moment to the next. Its time is measured in fractions of a second. A stream of impressions bombards our consciousness. In the desert, there is little to see apart from geological formations that have been shaped over millions of years and take centuries to change.

The heart of the desert beats at a different pace from ours. Geology can't be rushed. When it occupies your whole field of vision, you feel first impatience, then oppression, and finally that sense of calm that only a blank space can create. The stillness that only the absolute provides.

16

Uluru is an inverse Grand Canyon. The same red sandstone, the same grandeur. But the Grand Canyon, unlike Uluru, is instantly comprehensible. You can see its cause – the river – and understand at once how it came about. Uluru is a visual mystery, lacking any perceptible cause. A huge red shape lies gleaming at sunrise and sunset. Its bulk is out of proportion with everything around it. It just rises up out of the ground, unexpectedly and for no apparent reason.

In places some geological knife seems to have cut slices out of the rock walls. There are keyholes, cavities, perhaps stamps or emblems – or possibly brands denoting ownership, like on a bull. You expect it to rouse from its fossil sleep at any moment and come rushing at you. But it just lies there, not even shaking off the climbers who, like ants on an ant trail, toil upwards towards the bull's back.

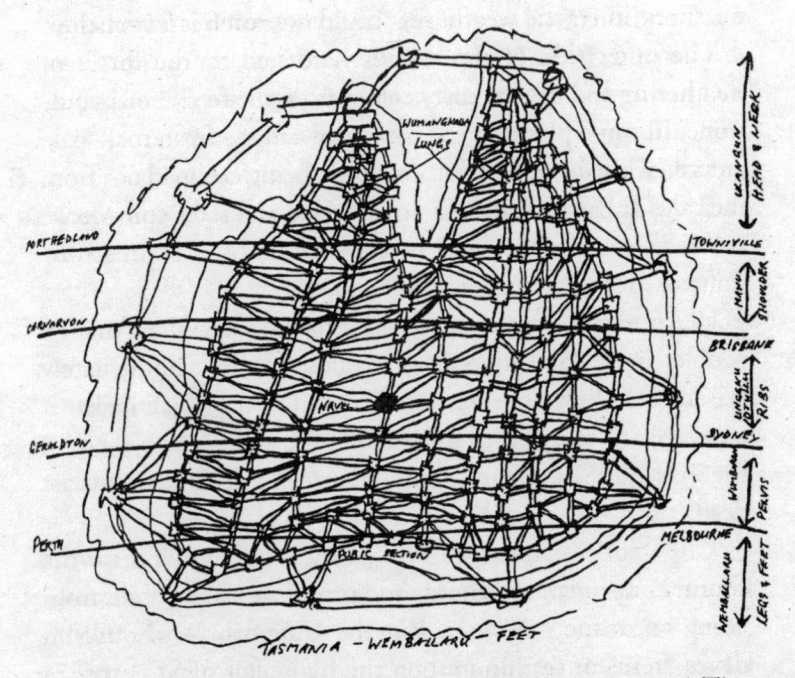

Bandaiyan, Australia as a human body with Uluru as the navel. The body is enclosed in a network of walking routes and mythical songlines. Drawing by David Mowaljarlai in Mowaljarlai and Malnic, *Yorro Yorro: Everything Standing Up Alive.*

Geologically speaking, Uluru is a so-called 'inselberg', an island in the surrounding flatness of the desert ocean.[16] The island consists of sandstone rich in feldspar, formed from a coarse gravel of gneiss and granite which came from the south about 600 million years ago. The Australian landscape is flat because it has been buried in the remains of its own geological decay. Why did this 'leftover mountain' survive when nearby mountains like it have weathered away and disappeared beneath the surface of the ground? One likely explanation is that Uluru was located at the top of a fold, where ground-water and chemical weathering could not reach it from below.

The outer skin of the rock is hardened by the forces of weathering and gets its rusty colour from the ferriferous sandstone. In some places in the caves you can see fresh rock, pale greyish-white or pink. Uluru is slowly being scooped out from the sides as the mountain is undermined and slabs come loose and fall. It is also suffering severe wear and tear from a continuous stream of ruthless climbers.

Uluru was 'restored' to its original owners, the Anangu people, in 1985. But only on condition they immediately leased back the whole area to a park authority which makes it accessible to tourists. Uluru has become a national symbol in the ever more aggressive marketing of Australia as a tourist destination.

Large notices announce that Uluru is holy ground for the country's original inhabitants and urge visitors to refrain from going on to the mountain. But the same people who would never dream of setting foot on the high altar of St Peter's in their heavy walking boots, or climbing the holy black stone in Mecca – those same people think it the most natural thing in the world to climb up Uluru and plant their boot on the bull's neck as if they had hunted it and brought it down. They imagine themselves conquerors, but at this distance they look more like dots on an Aboriginal painting.

17

Fortune seekers who saw the mountain glowing, or 'burning' believed they were seeing a mountain of gold, giving rise to endless myths and legends.

Ernest Favenc's *The Secret of the Australian Desert* (1896) was published in Swedish as part of the Fritzes Scout Library series, and I read it as a boy. It was my introduction to Australia.

It's a novel about three friends who set off into the desert in search of 'the burning mountain' and discover what lies behind 'this yarn the niggers have'. The question is: will the natives turn out to be peaceable, or will they offer resistance?

'However, it's safest to act as though they were our enemies.'

'Decidedly.'[17]

Beneath the bare ground, the sound of running rivers can be heard. 'There might be some Jinkarras living down there,' remarks Charlie. 'I wonder how this yarn of an underground race, the Jinkarras, originated.'[18]

Before long, they find a hole in the ground, through which they can see down to a cave beneath, where the Aborigines are sitting eating.

'The thing that puzzles me,' says Brown, 'is – what do these natives live on . . .? Within a hundred miles there isn't a feed for a bandicoot.'[19]

'It is meat they are eating, but what meat?'

Morton shudders at the question put to him. Truth flashes across his mind.

'An awful feeling of horror came over the whole party as they realized their situation and possible fate. Their natural audacity, however, soon returned. At present they were masters of the situation; with their breech-loaders they could shoot down a score of the natives helpless in the cavern below, if so inclined. But affairs did not seem to justify armed intervention just then.'

But a short time later, when they have forced their way into the cave and been witness to a human sacrifice, they open fire:

'"Fire like blazes," ordered Morton, setting an example which was followed by the others until the white smoke nearly filled the cavern. Madly and fanatically the natives dashed up the narrow passage; but with four breech-loaders playing on them, the terrible unknown lightning and deafening thunder smiting their foremost down, two and three at a time, the attempt was hopeless.'

The white men manage to get out just in time to avoid a convenient earthquake that fills the cave with scalding mud, burying the black men, dead and alive.

18

When the white men have calmed down somewhat, they start to question their intervention:

'After all we had no business – according to their ideas – to interfere with their little rites and ceremonies. They treated us in a friendly fashion.'

They even express passing concern about the outcome. The blacks are all dead. Only the chief is still alive, 'Scarred, bleeding and burnt, a most miserable object, the only survivor of his tribe.'[20]

'I cannot help feeling sorry for the old ruffian. He was a real plucky fellow.'

Cooper's *Last of the Mohicans* in a new guise. Yet another representative of nineteenth-century literature's romanticizing of 'the last of'. The extermination of native peoples was in full swing, while the great reading public wallowed in sympathy for the last one, the only man left.

The next time the group of white friends encounter the Aborigines, they know they are dealing with cannibals. So driving them away with firearms is not enough. 'Quick!' cries Morton. 'Not one must get away!'[21]

The men on horseback pull up beside a 'wounded savage'. Then, 'Morton slipped from his horse. Charlie turned his head away for he guessed what was going to happen. No quarter for the cannibals! He heard the revolver ring out. "Perhaps it is all for the best, sad as it seems," says Morton. "Those six devils could not have kept their lust for murder under."'

How did he know they were devils? Well, because the white men couldn't see enough food around to satisfy even a bandicoot, and because they couldn't see the animals hunted by the natives, or the grubs and roots they dug out of the sand, they assumed the natives must survive by eating each other. So the natives were cannibals, that is, devils who must be eradicated. That was their logic. Once the devils were gone, once the land had become no-man's-land, the deserts would turn into gardens.

'What a real desert!' exclaims Brown, gazing round on the dreary scenes.

'Yes, it's about as hopeless looking a picture as one could find anywhere, at present. No, burn this scrub off, or clear it somehow, and with a good supply of artesian water there are a hundred and one payable products one could grow here.'

'You are an optimist, Morton.'

'I am, as regards the future of Australia.'

19

Fiction at times came close to reality.

By the end of the nineteenth century, white settlers had taken over most of the land around Alice Springs. Their sixty thousand cattle and sheep ousted the Aborigines from the waterholes. Competition for water led to conflicts in which the Aborigines' spears were no match for the settlers' modern firearms. Killing a black was considered no worse than shooting a dog. The town's mounted policeman William Henry Willshire (1852–1925) threw the power of the police wholeheartedly behind the whites.[22]

In 1881 there were only five white women in the whole of central Australia. Twenty years later, there were still only nine white women in Alice Springs. Conflicts between whites and blacks became common as white men broke down ancient patterns of marriage and blurred the distinction between bride-buying, prostitution and rape.

Hardly able to contain his delight, Willshire recalls in his book *The Land of Dawning* (1896) how his police patrol happens on a 'beautiful maiden savage', who runs away screaming. She is caught, but attempts to escape during the

'Native policemen disperse the blacks'. Illustration from Lumholtz's *Among Cannibals*.

night by jumping into the river. The constable who apprehends her exploits her sexually until, as Willshire puts it, she is 'over head and ears in love with the tracker who caught her'.[23]

Reporting a white man for rape in Willshire's police station was not advisable.

The blacks were punished on the spot for their crimes; trials were considered unnecessary. No suspects were arrested, no reports were filed; the natives, guilty or innocent, were summarily dispatched.

One of the most violent punitive actions occurred at Owen Springs, south-west of Alice Springs. A white witness later reported that over 150 blacks were killed. The total number of black people killed during Willshire's time at Alice has been estimated at between five hundred and a thousand. The crime for which they were being punished was predominantly cattle-stealing. Willshire murdered human beings to protect cattle.

He boasted openly about what he had done, describing his massacres in a singular, baroque rhetoric:

At 3 o'clock we came upon a large mob of natives camped among the rocks. They scattered in all directions. It's no use mincing matters – the Martini-Henry carbines at the critical moment were talking English in the silent majesty of those eternal rocks. The mountain was swathed in a regal robe of fiery grandeur, and its ominous roar was close upon us. The weird, awful beauty of the scene held us spellbound for a few seconds.[24]

In February 1891 Willshire and his constables had, on some flimsy pretext, opened fire on sleeping Aborigines not far from the Temple Downs cattle station, killing two of them. This was done entirely as a matter of course. Afterwards the murderers were casually having breakfast with the settler, while his stock-men dragged away the bodies of the Aborigines and burnt them.

It proved to be the straw that broke the camel's back. The telegraph station manager, Frank Gillen, intervened in his capacity as magistrate and official Protector of the Aborigines. He went to the scene of the crime, heard statements from the witnesses, and then had Willshire arrested for murder. It was the first arrest made in all Willshire's time as a police officer at Alice Springs.

Willshire was taken to Port Augusta, where he spent several days under arrest while the cattle owners of Alice Springs collected £2,000 for his court costs. He was acquitted, of course, but transferred to another posting and eventually given early retirement. He ended his days as a night watch-man at the slaughterhouse in Adelaide, 'a post for which his career made him admirably qualified', to quote historian D. J. Mulvaney.

20

Willshire's reign of destruction was not unique. Similar crimes were being committed around the world: in Canada and the USA, in South America and South Africa, in North Africa and Siberia, in central Asia and central Australia – in fact wherever European settlers were in the process of taking land from its original owners. The extermination of the

Aborigines produced the no man's land which according to the doctrine of *terra nullius* gave the white settlers rights to the land.

Most whites were convinced that those who had been murdered in this way were members of an inferior race, doomed to destruction. They could cite the foremost biological authority of the day: Charles Darwin. In Chapters 5 and 6 of *The Descent of Man* (1871), he presents the extermination of indigenous peoples as a natural part of the process of evolution. Animal species have always exterminated one another; races of savages have always exterminated one another; and now that there are civilized peoples, the savage races will be wiped out altogether: 'When civilized nations come into contact with barbarians the struggle is short, except where a deadly climate gives its aid to the native race. At some future period, not very distant as measured by centuries, the civilized races of man will almost certainly exterminate and replace throughout the world the savage races.'[25]

Darwin had himself seen it happen – in Argentina, in Tasmania, in mainland Australia – and reacted strongly against what he saw. But in the context of his theory of evolution, the extermination of indigenous peoples no longer appeared a crime, but seemed to be the inevitable outcome of natural processes and the precondition for continued progress. Post-Darwin, it became the done thing to shrug one's shoulders at extermination. Those reacting with disgust were merely displaying their ignorance.

'Nothing can be more unscientific,' wrote George Chatterton Hill in his *Heredity and Selection* (1907), 'nothing shows a deeper ignorance of the elementary laws of social evolution, than the absurd agitations, peculiar to the British race, against the elimination of inferior races.' The truth is that the

British race, 'by reason of its genius for expansion, must necessarily eliminate the inferior races which stand in its way. Every superior race in history has done the same, and was obliged to do it.'[26]

'If the workforce of a colony cannot be disciplined into producing the profits rightly expected by the mother country,' writes Henry C. Morris in his *History of Colonization* (1900), 'the natives must then be exterminated or reduced to such numbers as to be readily controlled.'[27]

'The survival of the natives will only cause trouble,' wrote anthropologist George H. L.-F. Pitt-Rivers in his *The Clash of Cultures* (1927).

In fact, the Native Problem might well be defined as 'the problem created by the survival of those native races or their hybrid descendants that have not been exterminated by the "blessings of civilization"'. That is to say there is no native problem in Tasmania, and for the European population in Australia, the problem is negligible, for the very good reason that the Tasmanians are no longer alive to create a problem, while the aboriginals of Australia are rapidly following them along the road to extinction.[28]

Men like William Willshire practised what these theorists defended or even recommended. Since 1948 it has been known as 'genocide'.

In the same year that Ernest Favenc wrote *The Secret of the Australian Desert*, a large research team, the Horn Expedition, travelled the same route as the three friends in his story. The expedition report contains a collective portrait of 'the central Australian Aborigine' and what the scholars of the time knew about him:

> His origin and history are lost in the gloomy mists of the past. He has no written records and few oral traditions. In appearance he is a naked, hirsute savage, with a type of features occasionally pronouncedly Jewish ... He has never been known to wash. He has no private ownership of land, except as regards that which is not overcarefully concealed about his person ... Religious belief he has none ... he has no traditions and yet continues to practise with scrupulous exactness a number of hideous customs and ceremonies which have been handed from his fathers, and of the origin or reasons of which he knows nothing ... Thanks to the untiring efforts of the missionary and the stockman, he is being rapidly 'civilized' off the face of the earth, and in another hundred years the remaining evidence of his existence will be the fragments of flint which he has fashioned so rudely.[29]

The respect shown by John Eyre fifty years earlier has completely vanished. The scholars looks down on their subject with the unquestioned superiority of the occupying power.

When the natives deny the occupiers access to their records and traditions, scholarship declares that such do not exist.

When the appearance of the natives differs from the norm

among the occupiers, scholarship finds it an opportune moment for the airing of anti-Semitic prejudices.

When the natives adapt their hygiene to the lack of water and abundance of sand, scholarship sees merely an unwashed savage.

When the settler community has stolen the land from its original owners, scholarship finds that the natives have no land rights. And adds a jeering insult which shows a total lack of understanding of the natives' religious need for connection with the ground. Body paintings, ground paintings, myths, songs and dances – for the scholars they are nothing but 'hideous ceremonies' which the natives themselves do not understand.

This solid wall of white incomprehension ends with a death sentence couched in a tone of forced jocularity: they'll soon be gone. Soon, thank God, the problem will be disposed of for good. Soon the laws of biology will have made a reality of the fiction of *terra nullius*.

22

How did the recipients of this collective death sentence react?

After all, even a personal death sentence is hard to bear. So what must it feel like, living with the certainty that not only I myself but also everyone who speaks my language, lives as I do, believes as I do and hopes as I do, that our entire world will be wiped out, that our whole people will shortly die and there will be no one to come after us?

The leading men of the Arrernte people[30] didn't read the Horn report. But they got the message. They realized something had to be done. Somewhere they had to try to break through the wall of white incomprehension. They had to make at least some of the occupiers understand their beliefs, their society and their way of life.

Who? As manager of the telegraph station, Frank Gillen was one of the most powerful white men in the area. He had taken on the tyrant Willshire and won. He had long shown an interest in the culture of the occupied race. They had known him for almost two decades. They chose Frank Gillen.

Gillen, in his turn, chose Baldwin Spencer. He was a thirty-five-year-old biology professor from Melbourne, who arrived in Alice Springs with the Horn Expedition. It moved on after three days, but Spencer stayed for three weeks to listen to what Gillen had to tell him. Gillen had experience, local knowledge and local contacts. Spencer was educated, articulate and had international contacts. They complemented one another, and together the two partners became the Arrernte people's way out to the world.

Leading men of the Arrernte decided to allow Spencer and Gillen to witness a grand, seven-week cycle of ceremonies, which should really have taken place at Imanpa *en route* to Uluru but which was now moved to the back yard of the Alice Springs telegraph station to be easily accessible for the two researchers. From mid-November 1896 to 8 January 1897, Spencer and Gillen observed and documented an average of five or six ceremonies a day.

It has subsequently emerged that the ceremonies were carried out with many short-cuts and abridgements necessitated by the move to Alice and by the fact that many of the Aborigines who participated were not themselves members of the Arrernte people. Many misunderstandings also arose from the fact that the researchers didn't know the language and relied for the answers to their questions on interpreters speaking pidgin English.[31]

Baldwin Spencer took this photograph during a seven-week cycle of ceremonies in the telegraph station's back yard. He failed to realize he was part of one of the most successful publicity campaigns in history.

After Spencer had left, the Arrernte men carried on initiating Gillen into their secrets. He was soon able to send Spencer a further 110 pages of notes, which the latter incorporated into his field notes. Four months later, Spencer completed a summary, which was published in *Nature*. Through their two agents, the Arrernte people reached an international audience for the first time.

Spencer was also working on a book called *The Native Tribes of Central Australia*, which he finished in March 1898. Gillen read it and gave his comments chapter by chapter. The book was also read and edited in advance of publication by two of the leading ethnologists of the day, Edward Tylor and James Frazer. It was published on 13 January 1899 and caused an immediate international sensation.

'Since the publication of their first volume, half of the total production in anthropological theory has been based on their work and nine-tenths affected or modified by it,' wrote Malinowski in 1913.[32]

The men of the Arrernte had sung and danced for Gillen and Spencer and tried to explain the ideas embodied in their community and way of life. They only partially succeeded. Spencer retained a lifelong conviction that the Aborigines were a race doomed to extinction. He failed to notice that the natives he viewed as study objects were in fact using him as an instrument in one of the most successful publicity campaigns in history.

The Arrernte, an unknown desert people in the heart of the world's most remote continent, suddenly emerged as the best-known, most discussed natives in the world. They wouldn't let themselves be exterminated in silence. They were showing the world that their *terra* was not *nullius*.

The Alice Springs of today reminds me of Tamanrasset in the Sahara: the same dried-up riverbed running right through the town; the same road running south–north; the same feeling of huge distances in all directions; the same cosmopolitan character; the same sharp contrast between sun and shade, between white and black.

But Tam is that much dustier, poorer and tougher than Alice, which is a pleasant town, at least in winter. The winter climate is sunny and warm, with slightly chilly nights. I buy books in the Aranta Bookshop, run by two old ladies who treat the store as their living room and the customers as company. I buy a salad from Woolworths for my lunch, read Freud and Durkheim in the library, obtain maps from the Department of the Environment across the street, and have dinner sitting outside at the Sports Café, before going back to Alice Springs Resort on the other side of the bridge.

Alice is in permanent contact with outer space and the world metropolises. This remote spot in the desert is part of an international network that monitors all the satellite conversations, faxes and emails between the cities of the world. The American base for electronic espionage at Pine Gap has more than a dozen monitoring globes, which since 1970 have been picking up satellite signals from radio transmitters, telephones and radar all over the world. If a sigh is heard over a mobile phone anywhere on earth, it will also be heard in Alice Springs.[33]

The livelihood of the town depends on it. The base at Pine Gap owns more than six hundred houses in Alice and purchases £4 million worth of goods and services a year. That makes quite an impact in a little town of only twenty-five thousand people, and helps give it a white, middle-class feel.

The Aborigines make up just over 2 per cent of the population of Australia. But in the Northern Territory, they make up 30 per cent. The prophecy of the Aborigines dying out has not come true.

This is not because they are long-lived, in fact just the opposite. Life expectancy is just sixty for black men and sixty-six for black women. White people live on average seventeen years longer than black people.

No, it's the children that are causing the black proportion of the population to rise. The average age among Aborigines is twenty-one. An ageing white population is living side by side with an increasingly youthful black one.

At the office of the Discrimination Commissioner, the job is considered done: the official view is that there is no longer any discrimination against black people in Alice Springs.

'But then how can the unemployment be accounted for?' I wonder. 'And is there a place where white and black people meet on equal terms?'

The atmosphere between white people is open and friendly. People nod and say hello in typical small-town fashion. But a black person will never say hello unless the white person has offered a greeting first. Are they shy? Oppressed? Uninterested? Hostile?

Aborigines are to be found working in private and government offices, as shop assistants, cleaners and parking attendants, and as troublesome drunken layabouts in the parks. I see them as clients at court, as hospital patients, as artists in art galleries and occasionally as restaurant guests, usually in the company of white people. I see them in the library, reading, listening and watching videos. I practically never encounter an

Aborigine in any situation offering an opportunity or reason for 'meeting', 'talking', 'going for a coffee' or even acknowledging one another's existence. Strict rules demand advance written permission to visit an Aboriginal settlement, photograph an Aborigine or reproduce what an Aborigine says.

Why? Well, why should a long-despised people, now it is no longer faced with certain annihilation, go about longing to socialize with its former annihilators and despisers? Why should a long-exploited people be prepared to offer itself as an exotic, unpaid bait in the tourist traps?

24

That night, I dream that all the high ground in Stockholm is suddenly linked together by a system of light, slender footbridges.

I make my way on foot above the waters of Riddarfjärden from Mariahissen to Kungsklippan. I walk above the traffic of Götgatan, from Helgalunden to Sofia church. Another bridge links Sofia with Mosebacke, and Mosebacke with Mariaberget.

A spider's web of bridges, built of thin, pliable wood, covers the entire city. It is like that system of underground passages which in Charles Fourier's imaginary city links the workplaces and the lovers. What's more, the bridges afford wonderful views that make it a delight to walk up there, high above the time-and-profit-driven traffic.

The surprising combinations, the connections as swift and straight as a bird flies – each new bridge is hailed as a victory for reason and its imagination. All Stockholm is criss-crossed like a brain by these winding, airy gangways, where body moves as easily as thought.

25

How did human beings become human beings? That was the great question Darwin posed to his readers. If mankind was not created by God, but has gradually evolved from animal to human by natural selection, then which were the qualities in the animal that allowed it to become human?

Was it speed, strength and cunning in constant, life-or-death gladiatorial combat? Was it our ability to exterminate each other that made us human? That notion did feature in Darwin's work, and in the course of the second half of the nineteenth century it became increasingly prevalent in European consciousness under the name of 'Darwinism'.

But Darwin also offered an entirely different answer to this question. Mankind has achieved its current superiority over other species of animal above all by means of its social skills, its capacity for cooperation and mutual help. This aspect of Darwin's theory found its leading exponent in Petr Kropotkin.[34]

Kropotkin was a member of the Russian aristocracy, and became known for his expeditions to Siberia. There he went looking for examples of competition and combat between individuals of the same species, but instead found innumerable examples of cooperation. Cooperation is what enables weak animals to protect themselves against predators, look after their young and organize migration to new areas. Of course strength and speed are important for survival in certain circumstances. But cooperation is a far more significant factor in the battle for life, Kropotkin argued in his book *Mutual Aid: A Factor of Evolution* (1902).

Spencer was able to make a significant contribution to this discussion. He described the Arrernte people as 'naked, howling savages' unable to shape a clay pot, make a garment or appoint a chief. But they didn't remotely resemble the accepted 'Darwinian' picture of primitive man as violent, uncontrolled and interested only in gratifying his own egotistical urges.

Their religious life, as described by Spencer and Gillen, centred on 'Intichiuma', a ceremony to increase the food supply. The remarkable thing about it was that each clan would attempt to increase the supply of the plant or animal that the rules of taboo expressly forbade them to eat. Why invest so much ceremonial force to an end from which you could not yourself benefit? That was what James Frazer asked in a long letter to Spencer.[35]

And he gave the answer himself: although the individual clan cannot benefit from the results of its own Intichiuma ceremony, it will benefit from the results achieved by all the other clans. The combined effect of the efforts of all the clans will be an increased supply of food, from which all can profit.

Spencer and Gillen's Arrernte didn't live in the 'war of everyone against everyone'; they had a complicated system based on avoiding conflicts over food by extending family solidarity to an ever-growing circle of more and more distant relatives. They had strict marriage laws intended to minimize men's conflicts over women.

In short, Kropotkin's ideas were affirmed. Natural selection led not to combat and competition but to a quest for practices that avoid conflict. This applied to both animals and humans. Society already existed before human beings; but there were no human beings before society.

26

The most famous interpreters of Spencer and Gillen's data were Émile Durkheim and Sigmund Freud. Both used the Aborigines as windows on to the origins of human culture. Both took Darwin as their starting point. Like Darwin they wanted to create their own grand, comprehensive model of interpretation extending far beyond its original sphere. Freud saw himself as the Darwin of the soul, Durkheim as the Darwin of society.

Freud was born in 1856, Durkheim in 1858, Spencer in 1860. Spencer became a professor in Melbourne in 1887, the year in which Durkheim became a university lecturer in Bordeaux and Freud a doctor in Vienna. Durkheim published first: two epoch-making works of sociology in the mid-1890s. A few years later, Freud published the work with which he made his name, *Die Traumdeutung* (*The Interpretation of Dreams*, 1899), and Spencer's *Native Tribes* appeared the same year.[36]

Durkheim and Freud both grew up in poor Jewish families in which traditional religion and a close sense of community played a central role. Both of them abandoned the faith of their fathers but continued to feel its attraction throughout their lives. Both were fascinated by the primitive society described by Spencer and Gillen, in part because it resembled the narrow societies, driven by internal imperatives, in which they themselves had grown up.[37]

Durkheim's life's work culminated in *Les Formes élémentaires de la vie religieuse* (*The Elementary Forms of Religious Life*, 1912), a case study of the beliefs of the Arrernte people, seen as the most primordial and fundamental of all forms of religion and thus as the key to them all.

As the Australian Aborigine's ceremonies fill him with reverence and elate him to a state of rapture, he is not falling prey to delusions. Admittedly Durkheim takes the view that the Aborigine is mistaken in believing an animal or a plant is working the miracle within him. But no more than Durkheim's own father was mistaken when he believed it was Jahveh. The animal and Jahveh are merely metaphors for a genuine sensory experience, the experience of the society to which the believer belongs. A society capable of much more than the individual, a society that supports and helps the individual but also makes demands and administers punishments.

His whole study, writes Durkheim, is based on the conviction that the collective experiences of believers through the ages cannot be mere imagination. There is a 'religious experience' – but the very fact that believers at different times and in different parts of the world have had widely diverging perceptions of the basis of this religious experience makes it less likely that any one of them could be 'right'.

But the experience remains. There is a reality behind the articles of faith. That reality is society.

With this solution, Durkheim had reconciled himself with his father and the environment in which he grew up, and incorporated them into the new world of sociological concepts in which he was now living. He believed he had proved that what his father had spent a lifetime seeking, namely God, was identical to what he himself had devoted his life to studying: society.

27

In the autumn of 1896, when Spencer was in the back yard of the Alice Springs telegraph station observing the ceremonies that the theorists would subsequently interpret, Sigmund Freud's father had just died. The death of his father gave Freud the impetus to begin the self-analysis that would later become 'psychoanalysis'.

One of his core discoveries was that even as a child he had sometimes wished for his father's death. After a further ten years of analysing sons' desire to kill their fathers and marry their mothers, Freud was able to posit the 'Oedipus complex' as lying at the heart of all neuroses. And in *Totem und Tabu* (1912–13), patricide itself becomes, through a reinterpretation of Spencer and Gillen's data, the creative act that leads to the emergence of civilization.

Once again the central focus is the Arrernte people's Intichiuma ceremony. For Freud it is significant that the ceremony concludes with a feast at which it is permitted, indeed decreed, that the participants eat of their own totem animal, which at all other times is strictly taboo.

'Let us now envisage the scene,' Freud writes, giving his fantasy free reign.[38] The clan kills the totem animal and consumes it raw. During these proceedings, the clan members are dressed up as the animal they are eating and mimic its sounds and movements, as if to emphasize the identification of the humans with the animal. This act, individually forbidden to every participant, becomes obligatory when everyone does it together. No one is allowed to refuse. Once the totem animal has been consumed, it is mourned and tears are shed for it.

'Psychoanalysis has revealed to us that the totem animal is really a substitute for the father,' writes Freud. This leads to a hypothesis 'which may seem fantastic', he admits, but which establishes 'an unexpected unity among a series of hitherto separated phenomena'.

The Darwinian conception of the primal horde is dominated by a violent, jealous father who, wanting to keep all the females for himself, drives all his sons away. This primal state has never been scientifically observable anywhere. The most primitive societies we have observed, for example that of the Aborigines, consist of associations of men, within which all members are relatively equal. How, Freud asks, have these associations developed out of the primal state?

'By basing our argument upon the celebration of the totem, we are in a position to give an answer: one day the expelled brothers joined forces, slew and ate the father, and thus put an end to the father horde. Together they dared and accomplished what would have remained impossible for them singly.'

It seemed quite natural to these savage cannibals that the father should be consumed. By each eating part of the father's body, they were appropriating his strength for themselves. The totemistic feast at the Intichiuma ceremony, 'perhaps mankind's first celebration', became in that context a commemoration of the crime, the patricide, which gave rise to social organization, to ethics and religion.

For once the father is dead and eaten, the sons' hatred gives way to tenderness and contrite fear. 'The dead now became stronger than the living had been.' The brothers grow 'subsequently obedient' and forbid one another to kill or eat the father substitute, the totem animal. They also forbid one another to 'use' (as Freud puts it) the women made available by the killing of the father. The guilt-ridden brothers deny themselves the fruits of their crime as a way of seeking reconciliation with the dead father.

As Freud sees it, we still seek that reconciliation today. We seek it in holy communion when we consume the body and blood of Jesus in remembrance of the original totem meal, when the sons gorged themselves on the body of the dead primal father. We seek it in society and culture. Everywhere we seek to make amends for the original crime: the killing of the father. Freud ends his book with the assertion: 'In closing this study . . . I want to state the conclusion that the beginnings of religion, ethics, society and art meet in the Oedipus complex.'[39]

'Impressive,' said the mouse, when they told him the moon was made of green cheese.

28

These were truly impressive theoretical towers that Freud and Durkheim constructed with Spencer and Gillen's building bricks from the back yard of the telegraph station – without ever having been there, without even having seen an Aborigine.

They both based their work on fundamental assumptions that have proved incorrect. They believed the Arrernte people to represent a specific 'primitive' stage in human development, which other peoples had already passed. But there is no proof that all peoples develop in the same way, nor that the Arrernte people should be considered more 'primitive' than others.

On the contrary, the Arrernte are highly unusual, even by Australian standards; in particular, the ceremony that includes eating the totem animal is not found among other Aboriginal peoples. Bang goes the first half of Freud's hypothesis. Studies of the social life of primates don't bear out Darwin's belief in hordes dominated by a single, jealous male. Bang goes the second half.[40]

Durkheim ascribes to what Freud termed 'associations of men', and he himself termed 'clans', a role that in reality is played by other social groupings: the family (which lives together), the 'horde' of families (which sometimes live together) and the 'tribe' or 'people', who speak the same language and control a common territory. The clans, on the other hand, live scattered over wide areas, only meet on ceremonial occasions, and are not the social unit that Durkheim imagined. The 'society' he saw as the solid foundation underlying religious experience dissolves on closer inspection into a whole series of different 'societies'.[41]

And which of them merits the name of God?

To Kahlin Compound

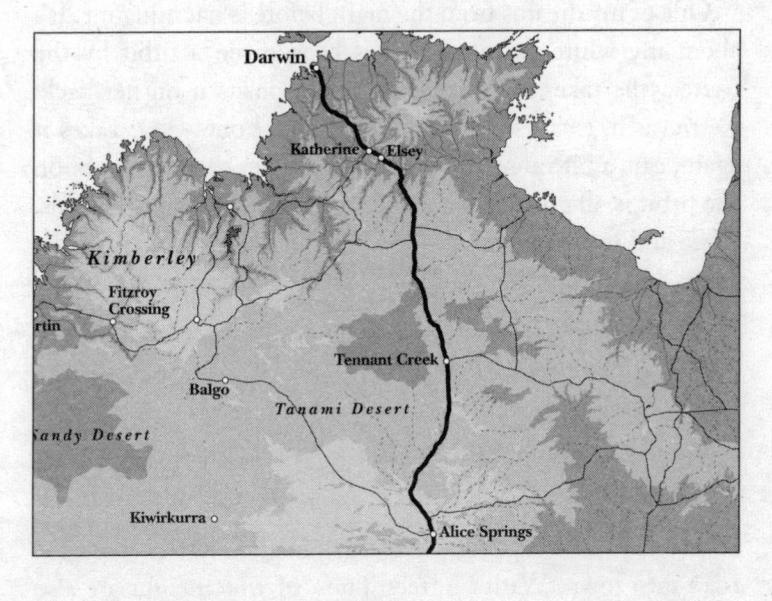

I'm driving north with the sun in my face (this being of course the southern hemisphere, where the midday sun is in the north). Just after Alice I pass the Tropic of Capricorn and am in the tropics. Red termite mounds rise from the ground and I'm surrounded on both sides of the road by whole copses of acacias, their flower spikes full of yellow pollen.

The road is so straight it's wearisome. I can see much further than the eye is able to see. Way off in the distance, beyond my range of vision, everything's lost in a hazy flickering. Even so, it's hard to keep your eyes off that point, since that's precisely where any danger would come from. No one drives with their lights on as they would in Sweden, and often the reflection of the sun on an oncoming vehicle is the first and clearest indication that it's there.

One of my dreams from the night before is haunting me. It's about my white parrot, who has been given a titbit by the waiter. She takes it in her beak and deposits it on her back. Retrieves it, eats a little and pops it under one wing. Takes it again, eats a bit more and pops it under her other wing. Soon the titbit is all gone. But the parrot has already forgotten this. Over and over she searches for it on her back and under her wings, but in vain. 'No titbit!' she shrieks desperately. 'No titbit!'

30

LIVE MORE! DRINK LESS! runs the slogan in giant letters above the road into town. With fourteen pubs, of which eight are also off-licences, Tennant Creek is the Australian town with the greatest density of drinking establishments. But it is also the town in which the Aborigines have declared war on alcohol.[42]

Most Aborigines in Tennant Creek don't drink alcohol. But those who do, drink too much. The drinkers are drawn to each other, so whole suburbs are laid waste by alcohol abuse. The children grow up without parents, and are alcoholics before they start school.

How did things get like this? Tennant Creek was once

called Junkurrarkur and was a holy site where the Warumungu
people's songlines and footpaths intersected. The whites built
a telegraph station there in 1872. White sheep farmers took
over the land. What little remained was set aside as an
Aboriginal reservation in 1892.

In 1932, a black boy called Frank Jupurrula found a nugget
of gold ten kilometres south of the telegraph station. Three
years later, a locust swarm of white prospectors had drained the
waterhole dry, destroyed the hunting and grazing grounds and
made the 'reservation' a joke. The booze flowed and prostitution became a major industry.[43]

In 1934 the anthropologist William Stanner discovered that
mining rights had been granted illegally inside the reservation
in some fifty cases, and that the telegraph station had five
hundred cows grazing on Aboriginal land, exploiting their
waterholes. The following year the reservation rights were
simply annulled, and the Warumungu people forced to move
forty kilometres north to Manga Manda, notorious for its
scorpions, red spiders and perpetual water shortage. Twenty
years after that, the Warumungu were moved on again, to Ali
Curung, far from their traditional lands.

The reason for these repeated moves was the need to evict the
Aborigines from land that had become valuable. The thinking
was, too, that desert people, as nomads, should be used to moving
around. In actual fact, the enforced transportation and accommodation in camps destroyed their original lifestyle. For many,
only drink remained. 'We walked to paradise – Wycliff Well
Hotel. It was a long way. But we walked for that grog.'[44]

Times got even worse at Tennant Creek when the abattoir
closed and mining declined. The population shrank from
9,000 to 3,500. Pubs and liquor stores lost a large proportion
of their customers. To stay in business, the pubs began offering

credit. The first drinks were free of charge, but the pub owners charged all the more once the customer was drunk.

In the 1990s, the Aborigines started a campaign against the pubs. The whites don't shoot us any longer, they poison us with liquor. They've always wanted to be rid of us. Alcohol is just the latest ploy for achieving a *terra nullius*. The unregulated sale of alcohol in Tennant Creek, according to the Julalikari Council, is 'a state sanctioned act of genocide against Aboriginal people'.[45]

The Julalikari Council represents Aborigines from sixteen different language groups in ten different suburbs. The programme of the organization has four main points:

The fight against drug abuse
Education and employment
Land and housing
Culture and traditions.[46]

The first point is seen as critical for the other three. The demand is for stricter control of when alcohol can be served. The pub owners should not serve customers who are spilling their drinks and having trouble finding their mouths. Alcohol should not be sold on credit. One day each week should be alcohol-free, preferably the day pensions and social-security benefits are paid out. The council is also demanding a tax on alcohol to finance the treatment of the victims of alcoholism.

On the way home, beneath the pink neon lights of the main street, I pass the Fernandez Bar and Restaurant, which entices customers with 'shooters' at $6 a shot: 'Slippery Nipple', 'Blow Job', 'Cock Sucking Cowboy' and 'Orgasm'.

The pub war continues. Above the road out of town flutters the slogan DRINK LESS! LIVE MORE!

Cool morning turns into hot afternoon. I've passed the 'tick limit', where the cattle used to have to be dipped before they could be taken any further; I've passed the palm limit and the limit for rainy-season flooding. The copses have grown into forests: the patches of green have spread and cover the ground entirely.

A century ago, Elsey was a remote cattle station which Jeannie Gunn wrote into Australian hearts with her two best-selling books, *The Little Black Princess of the Never-Never* (1903) and *We of the Never-Never* (1908). Today it lies just a few tarmacked kilometres from the main highway.

The little black princess is Mrs Gunn's maidservant. 'She didn't sit – like fairy-book princesses – waving golden sceptres over devoted subjects, for she was just a little bush nigger girl or "lubra", about eight years old. She had, however, a very wonderful palace – the great lonely Australian bush.'

The tone of the tale, familiar, intimate, jocular, is established from the outset. 'It takes a good deal of practice to tell a King at a glance – when he is naked and pulling up weeds.'[47] The white people call the king Goggle Eye: 'He was very proud of his "white-fellow name", as he called it. You see he didn't know what it meant.' Little jokes like this at the expense of black people are all part of the kindly, condescending attitude. They are portrayed as childishly pathetic and comical. The reader is invited to admire their tracking abilities, while laughing at their poor English and defective arithmetic. Contradictory generalizations abound: on one page we read that no 'black-fellow' can count beyond two; on the next the 'black-fellow' knows unerringly how many eggs are laid by different bird species.[48]

This is a charming children's book with no violence in it. But it's still assumed that you don't leave the house unarmed. When the white people mark the coronation of King Edward with a gun salute, the black people are panic-stricken; they throw down the flour and syrup and run away. 'We shouted to them to stop and said we were only having a "playabout"; but they did not wait to hear. We ran after them, but that only made matters worse.'[49]

The incident is related as an example of the comic misunderstandings that can arise between white and black people, and of black people's laughable lack of courage and self-control. But why were they so scared? Did they perhaps have good reason for taking fright? What had experience taught them about drunken white men firing revolvers? Mrs Gunn doesn't so much as touch on the subject.

32

For all its defects, *The Little Black Princess* was Australian literature's first full-length portrait of a young black girl.[50] It took another half-century for the first autobiography of a black woman to be published: *Tell the White Man: The Life Story of an Aboriginal Lubra* (1949).

Readers immediately know where they are when Buludja describes her childhood on the ranch: it's Elsey Station in Mrs Gunn's time. 'She was the first white lubra I had known and I well remember her arrival.'[51] Buludja hides under the veranda so she can listen to the whites and learn their language. She is old King Goggle Eye's favourite. She has a playmate and best friend called Taclammah. They go to bathe at sunset every day. A hundred little details link the two works. Behind the first literary character and the first autobiography we sense the same black woman: Buludja.

Her story is far less idyllic than Mrs Gunn's. She tells of killing her first two children: 'I did not want any children. They would be a nuisance . . . As soon as it was born I closed its nostrils between two fingers and held my hand over its mouth so that it could not breathe . . . It was much easier to get rid of the baby than have the trouble of looking after it . . . A few years later I had a new baby which I smothered as soon as it was born.'[52]

Her employer finds out what is happening and worries about the future labour supply for his station. He decides that from then on, every newborn baby's arrival will be celebrated with the slaughter of an ox, and the baking of bread using a whole sack of flour. The little children will even come to the main house to be fed bread and milk. 'So I killed no more.' Buludja bore five children, of which three survived.

So the first time a black woman has a chance to give an account of her life, she admits having murdered two of her children out of sheer laziness, and having stopped the killing only as a result of her white employer's resourceful intervention.

One small problem remains. It wasn't Buludja herself who recorded her story. It was done by her employer, H. E. Thonemann, whose name is also given as author of the book. It's true he claims to have kept faithfully to Buludja's story and described everything from her perspective. But he often forgets himself and sees things from a white, male point of view. It's conceivable that he saw his own steps to prevent infanticide as more important than they really were. It's even possible he was duped.

The first time infanticide is mentioned, it's with reference to 'light-coloured piccaninnies', that is, children of black mothers and white fathers. If anyone gives birth to such a child and doesn't kill it, the police can come and take it away, Buludja says. 'We do not understand why they should take our pic-caninnies away from us and never let us see them again. They tell us it is the white man's law. We do not like our children being taken away from us, so sometimes we hide and some-times we kill them.'[53]

These are the words of another kind of mother, not an indo-lent girl who can't be bothered to look after her babies, but a mother who wants at any price to stop the police getting the child. What is she to say? If she says, 'I've hidden it,' it's an invitation to the police to carry on looking. If she says, 'I've killed it,' perhaps she'll be able to keep it.

33

Why were the police on the lookout for fair-skinned children? Well, at the beginning of the twentieth century white society was concerned about the growth in the number of so-called 'half-castes'. It was becoming increasingly common for white men to have children with black women, and then play no part in their upbringing. There could be no question of forcing white men to take responsibility for their 'illegitimate' chil-dren, so the children were to be removed from their black families and put in institutions. The justification given for the policy was as follows: 'The half-caste is intellectually above the aborigine, and it is the duty of the State that they be given a chance to lead a better life than their mothers. I would not hesitate for one moment to separate any half-caste from its aboriginal mother, no matter how frantic her momentary grief might be at the time. They soon forget their offspring.'[54]

So the police hunt for fair-skinned children was undertaken in part for the children's own good, in part to make the best use of the valuable gene pool the white men left behind them in the Aboriginal camps. Taking the children into custody would also contribute to the final solution of the race question. White society spoke in terms of 'breeding out' the blacks, rather than killing them off by shooting them. Making black women bear fair-skinned children who were immediately confiscated and incorporated into white society would hasten and facilitate the process of black extinction.

In the Northern Territory, the Aboriginals' Ordinance of 1911 gave a protector, appointed by the whites, blanket authority to take into custody any Aborigine or 'half-blood' whenever he considered it expedient. The ordinance came into force when Baldwin Spencer was Protector of the Aborigines. He wrote: 'No half-caste children should be allowed to remain in any native camp, but they should all be withdrawn and placed on stations . . . even though it may seem cruel to separate the mother and child, it is better to do so, when the mother is living, as is usually the case, in a native camp.'[55]

The ordinance remained in force until 1957; yet the number of children in custody didn't start to decline until the 1970s. It was only in 1995 that a national inquiry was set up, and exposed the full extent of the crime.

When I was little, I was taught to call every adult man 'uncle'. It was usual in those days, and nobody took it as proof that every adult male really could be my father's brother, or that my paternal grandmother had practised group sex.

My grandmother was a member of the Betania mission society, where it was customary for people to call each other 'brother' and 'sister'. This habitual form of address didn't give rise to any hypotheses about the congregation engaging in group sex, either.

But when the wealthy American businessman Lewis Henry Morgan found out that certain North American Indians called each other 'brother' and 'sister', he was prompted into novel and titillating trains of thought.[56] Perhaps, Morgan speculated, this is a form of address surviving from an earlier era when everyone of the same generation could be biological brothers and sisters because their parents lived in group marriages and practised group sex.

Maybe, Morgan conjectured further, this didn't only apply to a specific group of Indians. Perhaps all primitive peoples had at some early phase of their development lived in group marriages, the women belonging not to a single man but to all the men in the group.

Seeking evidence for his thesis, Morgan sent a questionnaire to places all round the world, and received an answer from a missionary in Australia. The latter reported that some Aboriginal women used the same form of address for their husband's brother as they did for him. They called them all the equivalent of 'my husband'. This was conceivably a practice surviving from a bygone era when brothers owned all their women in common.

The idea that humankind had originally lived in a state of sexual communism was transmitted on from Morgan's *Ancient Society* (1877) via Karl Marx, who read the book and noted down extracts from it in his final years, 1881–2, to Friedrich Engels, who found Marx's notes after his death and used them as the basis of his *Der Ursprung der Familie, des Privateigentums und des Staats* (*The Origin of the Family, Private Property and the State*, 1884).

Engels begins with an enthusiastic account of Morgan's ideas, including the idea that for some Aboriginal peoples marriage is a union of two groups rather than two individuals. For Engels, this assertion applies not to some hypothetical prehistoric age but to current and continuing practices.

In fact, Engels sees group marriage as the key to the process of becoming human.[57]

The human animal would never have survived without its capacity for interfamily cooperation. The most serious obstacle to this suprafamilial organization was jealousy. The transition from animal to human occurred when the males abandoned their claim to sexual monopoly and started sharing females between them. Human beings only became human by means of an uninhibited sex life in a society where all the adult men and women belonged to each other.

This was something of which my grandmother was blissfully unaware.

Those who introduced the Aboriginals' Ordinance of 1911 had certainly never read Morgan, Engels, or their many successors. But the hypotheses and speculations of those theoreticians seeped into society in the form of rumours of loose living and group sex. The rumours hardened into prejudice: black women would have sex with a man as soon as look at him, and didn't know who the fathers of their children were. Thus they couldn't love their children, so they killed or mistreated them. It was a blessing for the children to be saved from the sexual snakepit where they had been born, and where they would soon be forgotten again.

35

In 1913, all Europe was discussing the indigenous peoples of Australia. It was among those peoples that all the theory merchants – Morgan and Engels, Frazer and Spencer, Kropotkin, Durkheim and Freud – hoped to find the point at which human beings became human. It was there they sought the origins of civilization, the cradle of culture, the birth of society, the roots of religion. Then along came a young Polish anthropologist called Malinowski and turned everything on its head, with his thesis *The Family Among the Australian Aborigines* (1913).

He differed in two crucial respects from all who went before.[58]

First, he questioned the search for a primal state. He rejected the validity of the very question that everyone else was trying to answer. He doubted that all humans had passed through the same stages in the course of their development. Conditioned by their climate and their environment, the Aborigines created social institutions exerting mutual influence over each other. Their society is worth studying for its own sake – not as a preliminary stage of Europe, but as one of many potential solutions to the basic problems common to all humankind.

Second, he maintained that a critical approach to sources is as vital for the ethnographer as it is for the historian. He takes as an example the assertion 'It is the group which marries the group and begets the group.'[59] To whom does this refer? A particular Aboriginal people, all Aborigines, or perhaps all primitive peoples? Does it apply to the present, the past, or primeval times? How does the source know this? Personal observation? Second- or third-hand account? In which language? What are the language skills of the parties? Who was the interpreter? What interests did the narrator have in the matter? The interpreter? The researcher? How did his theory influence his gathering of facts? And so on.

After this scrutiny of the evidence, nothing much remained of the original assertion. Sexual infidelity, yes of course. That occurs in most societies. A man with several wives, yes, frequently. But no one has ever seen 'the group which marries the group and begets the group', and the circumstances which led to that conclusion have other, far more likely explanations.

Once the source material has been immersed in this acid bath, what is actually left of our knowledge of the family life of the Aborigines? Do we know anything definite at all? What are emotional relations between parents and children like, for example? Do the parents care for the children?

Yes, replies Malinowski, on that point all the sources are unanimous. Conflicting observations are made on other questions, but when it comes to parental love, the sources all agree. The observations are concrete. Parents are kind to children who need help, and show great patience with them. Both fathers and mothers look after their children conscientiously, and very seldom punish them.

There are innumerable accounts testifying to parents' love

for their children. A father exposes himself to mortal danger to rescue his son. A mother is a broken woman as she mourns her son. A man searches desperately for his lost son (despite claims that individual paternity doesn't exist among his people). In these accounts, it's never a group of fathers and mothers anxious or grieving or risking their lives – it's always the individual mother or father of a specific child.

Malinowski established that all that was really known about the family life of the Aborigines in 1913 was that they love their children and are deeply attached to them. Simultaneously, a policy was being introduced in Australia that was to take tens of thousands of children from their black parents, brothers and sisters, on the grounds that black parents don't really care about their children: 'They soon forget their offspring.'

36

Aboriginal children grew up in great freedom, loved and cherished. White Australians had often known very different childhoods. Most came from Great Britain. Many remembered a childhood of hard work, sleeping on the factory floor under the machines. Others remembered a childhood without parents, abandoned in bullying boarding schools. How did they react when they saw black children growing up unpunished, surrounded by loving parents, siblings and other relatives?

Even Malinowski couldn't resist raising a warning finger to the Aborigines for not beating their children. He saw it as a shortcoming in their child-rearing methods, 'for it is impossible to conceive of any serious education without coercive treatment'.[60]

Other whites must have reacted even more sharply to what they perceived as laxity in Aboriginal children's upbringing. What a provocation the Aborigines' whole lifestyle, particularly their interaction with their children, must have been to the British! A childhood without shame, without guilt, without punishment! Surely a great sense of loss must have welled up inside them, a sense of missing all these things they were now condemning as neglect, defective hygiene, lack of manners and discipline. When they took fair-skinned children from their black mothers, was it because those children were getting something they themselves had never had, and they felt a bitter sense of lack when they saw others getting it?

The matter came to a head when a white father and a black mother lived together and two widely differing notions of child-rearing had to be reconciled. We get a glimpse of the conflicts that could then arise in Catherine Martin's classic novel *An Australian Girl* (1890).

Old Thompson, on his deathbed, tells the story of the biggest mistake of his life.[61] He had heard that a half-caste inherits the worst qualities of both races, so he would anxiously scan his son by a black woman called Caloona for any sign of negative traits. The boy was sharp, all right, and so funny his parents fell about laughing. But whenever his father tried to teach him manners, he would play dumb or start crying, and his mother's hands would tremble. One day, when the boy was seven, he let a young dog loose among the newborn lambs.

I took him by the hand to the hut, and before punishing him
I asked him why he did such a thing. His mother stood there

shiverin', looking at us, and the boy burst out cryin' and
denied it hard an' fast. He said he was callin' the dog off. This
riled me so much that on the instant I give him a bad
thrashin' – worse, I know, nor I should have – so that the
mother turned on me very fierce like. I got into a bad Scot,
an' told her if she did not let me bring up the boy proper she
had better clear. In course, I never meaned a word of it, and
never thought as Caloona would take it to heart. But the boy
sulked and would eat no food, an' made believe he was very
badly hurt. God knows, perhaps he was, though I didn't
believe a word of it, an' felt very hard agin him for telling such
barefaced lies. Next day his mother stayed in the hut with
him and wouldn't even look at me when I was going out.
When I came home that night they were both gone, an' from
that day to this I never set eyes on them.

37

Children's fear of being separated from their parents, parents'
dread of losing their children – these are universal human feelings occurring in all times and cultures. But in one particular
place, Australia, and at one particular time, the second half of
the nineteenth century, literary fiction becomes obsessed with
the subject of 'the lost child', writes Peter Pierce in his book
Country of the Lost Children: An Australian Anxiety (1999).

The definition of lost children in this context is: 'Boys and
girls of European origin who strayed into the Australian
bush'.[62] The literature of the period is full of stories of children
who disappear, their courage and fortitude, their hunger, thirst

and other sufferings, their parents' despair and frantic search, and the children's eventual rescue or doom.

Why? The aim of the stories, it was said, was to warn young children against going off on their own or straying too far from home. But the intense preoccupation with this theme has far deeper roots, according to Pierce.

He sees the lost child as symbolic of an Australia peopled by lost Englishmen who, finding themselves on the other side of the globe, felt too far from England and were afraid they'd never find their way back home. They felt lost in a '*terra nullius*' that belonged neither to them nor to anyone else. They imagined themselves forgotten and abandoned by their mother country, and expressed those emotions in stories about lost children.

That, at least, is Pierce's interpretation. It makes him limit his investigation to white children and white parents, since Aborigines would hardly have gone around longing to be back home in England. It makes him end his investigation of the motif at the start of the twentieth century, when Australia became independent.

In other words, he breaks off his investigation of the 'lost child' theme at the very moment when children really did begin to disappear – not just a few odd cases, but wholesale, in their thousands and tens of thousands, not by mistake or by accident, but as a deliberate result of a federal and state policy voted through by the settler democracies.

How was the disappearance of Aboriginal children reflected in literature? Was their resilience and heroism somehow different from that of the white children? Were their black mothers indifferent to their loss or did they experience the same hopelessness and despair as white mothers? Pierce doesn't tell us.

If dread of losing children was a white Australian obsession in the second half of the nineteenth century, might that have been one motivation for starting to steal black people's children, forcing them to experience the same dread, the same nightmares, that the whites had suffered for a quite different reason? Might their underlying aim have been that of freeing themselves from their own dread by transferring it to the others, to black people?

Questions of this kind are totally absent from Pierce. He shuts up shop in 1900 and opens for business again in 1950, with a punctuality that enables him to ignore completely how the systematic abduction of fair-skinned Aboriginal children is reflected in fiction, if it all.

38

One of the remarkable novels to fall into Pierce's void is Catherine Martin's *The Incredible Journey* (1923). The writer was seventy-five when she broke a long silence with one last book. Why did she write it? Perhaps because the state of South Australia, where she lived, was about to implement the Better Protection, Care and Control of Aboriginal Children Act, which would extend the state's powers to take children of black mothers into custody.

Martin takes us to an Aboriginal camp by the fictional Jane Creek, close to 'the naked heart of Australia'. The Aborigines speak the Arrernte language. A short distance away there is a grand house, whose white inhabitants know what it means to lose a child. Two of their own had gone astray in the forest, and it was only with the aid of the Aborigines' tracking skills that they were found and brought home. Thus far, the story adheres to the nineteenth-century model: if lost children are found, it is nearly always by black trackers.

But then comes something new. A white man, Simon, kidnaps a twelve-year-old black boy, Alibaka, and takes him far off into the desert, where he's completely in Simon's power. His mother, Iliapa, is initially paralysed by the loss of her son. 'She lay stone-still, unable to shed a tear.'[63] But the next morning she meets her friend Polde, who has already crossed the desert once. Together they set out on foot to try to track down the boy. The 'incredible journey' begins.

The two black women are depicted neither as comic and helpless, nor as infanticidal monsters, but as adult human beings who know what they are doing and are able to make use of their exceptional range of talents. They find snakes and lizards to eat, and know where to dig their sticks in to find water; they keep well away from men, black and white, and enter into alliances with women, black and white. They survive a sandstorm by rolling up all their belongings close beside them and lying face down. They locate water by watching the flight of birds. At length, they reach the (fictitious) town of Labalama, where the boy is being held prisoner by Simon, a short, fat man with a face the colour of old brick.

"'This is my mother who has come for me.'", says Alibaka proudly.

"'The cheek of niggers! Do you really mean to tell me that you think you are going to take this boy away from me?'"

"'That is why I come.'"[64]

The police side with the white man and decide the boy should stay with Simon until Iliapa can prove she's the child's mother – however she's supposed to do that. The days go by;

nasty bruises appear on the boy's face, and Iliapa realizes he's being beaten. She's on the verge of giving up. But through a combination of furious love and skilful diplomacy, she finally gets the better of the white man.

Catherine Martin returns to the theme of 'the lost child', but puts a black woman at its heart. The book was bound to cause an indignant outcry among many white readers. Martin knew this, as is obvious from both her preface and her narrative tone. But it would have been 'a sort of treachery', she writes, to leave the black women's side of the story untold. 'A fellow can't be allowed to steal a child from a black mother any more than from a white one.'[65]

39

In the second half of the twentieth century, the lost child of literature gives way to 'the abandoned child'. Instead of hunting frantically for their lost children, parents (according to Pierce) try in every conceivable way to get rid of their offspring. But here Pierce, once again as a result of the limitations he has imposed on his study, misses the most important piece of evidence for proving his thesis.

Xavier Herbert's *Capricornia* (1938) marks the breakthrough of modern literature in Australia. It tells of two brothers who shortly after the turn of the century arrive in the town now known as Darwin. Oscar dresses in white, moves in the best circles and rises up in the world. Mark finds himself in bad company, drinks to excess and fathers a child with a black woman.

On a downy sheet of paper-bark beside her lay a tiny bit of squealing, squirming honey-coloured flesh. Flesh of his own flesh. He set down the lantern, bent over his son. Flesh of his flesh – exquisite thing! He knelt. He touched the tiny heaving belly with a fore-finger. The flesh of it was the colour of the cigarette-stain on his finger. Smiling foolishly he said with gentle passion, 'Oh my lil man'.

The thought of anything bad happening to his son makes him rigid with fear. 'S'pose some feller hurtim belong me piccanin. I'll kill every blunny nigger in the camp. Savvy?'[66]

But once the initial joy of fatherhood wears off, he loses interest and leaves. Some years later, he finds his son playing with an emaciated mongrel dog. The child's mother is dead; people call him Noname.

'He was unutterably filthy. Matter clogged his little eyes and nose; his knees and back and downy head were festered; dirt was so thick on his scaly skin that it was impossible to judge his true colour; and he stank.'[67]

Mark is filled with remorse. He tells a woman to wash the child. He gives him food and clothing. Soon the boy's eyes no longer look like those of a hunted animal. He grows 'fat and bold and beautiful'.

But then Mark is away for a year, and on his return he has a new black woman, who drives Noname away. What the boy doesn't learn from his mother's people, he learns from the dogs.

The years pass, and the next time Mark meets his abandoned son, Noname has virtually turned into a wild animal. Mark catches the boy and sells him as a slave to his friend Jock.

Mark's successful brother Oscar has bought a cattle station, and Jock decides one day to send Noname there because he has become too difficult. His howls of misery are keeping the dogs awake at nights. The author's alter ego, Peter Differ, tries to persuade Oscar to keep the boy:

'Don't send the kid to the Compound, Oscar. It will mean the ruin of him. He'll grow up to learn nothing but humility ... Think of the life before the kid ... Life-long humiliation. Neither a white man nor a black. A drifting nothing.'[68]

Oscar is increasingly charmed by the boy; he says his parents are dead, and adopts him.[69]

40

Peter Differ drinks himself to death, and from his deathbed sends his beautiful 'half-caste daughter' Connie to the local Protector, begging him to take care of her. The Protector, whose duty is to protect the interests of the Aborigines, promptly gets her pregnant. He promises that if she never tells anyone who the father of her child is, he will come and fetch her and they will live happily ever after. Connie, alone with the child, becomes just one more black prostitute along the railway.[70]

One day, railway worker Tim O'Cannon comes along the rails on his inspection trolley.

He trundled on, up grade and down, through dripping cuttings where golden catch-fly orchids grew in mossy nooks and tadpoles wriggled in sparkling pools, over culverts where smooth brown water sped over beds of grass, past towering walls of weeds that stretched out leaves and flowers to tickle his face and shower him with dew and touch him – as though he were a flower to be fertilized – with blobs of pollen.[71]

In the midst of this paradise, he suddenly sees a white child. And there at the foot of the railway embankment lies Connie. 'She was lying on a bed of leaves, clad only in a sugar bag, thin as a skeleton, black with filth and flies.'

'She began to cough. She coughed till her body heaved, till dust was flying from her wretched bed, till it seemed her poor thin frame must burst into leatherly fragments, till she fell back gasping, with tears streaming from her eyes, bloody spittle from her mouth.'

He takes her to the compound. When he goes to see her the next day, the doctor still has not been. Whaddya mean, sick and dying? This is no proper woman, just a half-caste whore, so why are you making such a fuss, Mr Busybody?

Connie is put in isolation in the venereal-disease ward. They say she will die within a few days. Tim creeps in at night and rescues her little daughter Tucky.

Shortly afterwards, Tim has a fatal accident during one of his heavenly trolley rides. His whole family, including Tucky, ends up in the compound.

41

Today, Kahlin Compound in Darwin is just an empty building site by the beach, where Gilruth Avenue crosses the road to Myilly Point. This is where Baldwin Spencer set up a camp under his protectorate in 1913 for the collection and holding of Aborigines. In those days it was out of sight of the town itself, but still close enough to provide an easily accessible labour supply for the town's middle class. Soon they began to sort them into 'half-bloods', who were kept, and 'full-bloods', who were moved on to other camps further away.

A committee formed in 1923 found that public opinion in Darwin demanded the 'half-castes' be taken from their native parents at the earliest opportunity, to be 'reared in a more healthy and elevating environment'. But people did not want them in the town itself, where they constituted 'a danger to health' and exerted 'an undesirable influence on white children'. The challenge was to isolate the 'half-castes' from their black families and from white children whilst keeping them accessible to white employers.[72]

Once the fair-skinned Aboriginal children had been separated from their parents, they were to have their native identities scraped away. The children were to be trained, the boys learning handicraft skills and ranching, the girls housework. At fourteen they would be sent out to work, unpaid, in order to learn their place in the lowest stratum of white society. In practice, there was never enough money for anything except keeping the children locked up and sending them to work.

Xavier Herbert spent six months in Darwin in 1927–8, where he came into contact with racism in its most virulent form. He met a postman who had a little black boy as his 'gate opener' and kept him chained under the postcart at nights to stop him running away. He met Dr Cecil Cook, who wanted to solve the Aboriginal problem by means of eugenics. All Aboriginality was to be bred out by pairing 'half-caste' women with suitable white men – a method crudely known as the 'fuck 'em white policy'.[73]

During his first stay in Darwin, Herbert met most of the people who later featured in his first novel. The book was virtually finished when he returned to Darwin in 1935 as the acting superintendent of Kahlin Compound. The camp was in a sorry state and Herbert was obliged to begin by installing latrines and organizing school classes. He soon found himself in conflict with other authorities locally, because he defended the Aborigines and identified with their problems in a way that the whites in power found intimidating. Herbert's provisional appointment was not renewed.[74]

'The Compound' is the geographical and emotional centre around which everything in *Capricornia* revolves. The novel was published in 1938. Kahlin Compound was closed down in 1939.

42

Twelve years after his adoption Noname, now called Norman, qualifies as an engineer at the technical university in Melbourne, where nobody cares about the colour of his skin. But when the time comes for him to return to Oscar on the station, he gets no further than the ticket window before attitudes start to change. He gets a cabin right in the stern of the boat. He notices his fellow passengers leaving him more and more alone, the further north the boat gets. He disembarks and is addressed as 'nigger'.

He's able to laugh it off. But once he gets to Darwin, he's

spoken to in pidgin English in spite of his dazzling white suit and the university diploma in his pocket, and is asked to wait outside. It isn't funny any more.

Rejected by the whites, Norman is drawn to the Compound and meets Tucky, now fourteen. Always hungry, she sneaks out at night to look for crabs on the beach. She gets found out and is sent to a mission station. When she runs away, the police hunt her right across the state. Norman hides her in a disused water cistern on his cattle station. The missionaries find her, pregnant, and demand that Norman marry her. But the Protector does not approve the marriage: 'Norman was disqualified because of his "superiority to the girl".' So she is to be returned to the Compound.

Norman is beside himself: 'What's she got to grow up to? I'll tell you, all of you, you pale-faced cows – to be a coloured slave to high and mighty whites – to the likes of you that can be masters just because your faces are damn well white – to be humble – to keep her place – to . . . to . . .'.[75]

This outburst costs Norman three months in jail. Tucky is waiting for him when he returns to the cattle station. When the police turn up once more, Norman thinks they have come for the heavily pregnant Tucky, and tells her to hide. But this time it's him they are looking for. He is taken away, accused of murder, and only released after an extended trial.

Back at the station, ruined by the cost of the trial, he sees two crows flying up out of the old cistern.

Dry grass rattled against the iron. Dry wind moaned through rust-eaten holes. He stepped up to the tank and peeped through a hole. Nothing to see but the rusty wall beyond. He climbed the ladder, looked inside, saw a skull and a litter of bones. He gasped. A human skull – no – two – a small one and a tiny one. And human hair and rags of clothes and a pair of bone-filled boots. Two skulls, a small one and a tiny one. Tucky and her baby!

Thus the story ends. The once abandoned child Noname finds the abandoned child Tucky, daughter of the abandoned child Connie, and his own abandoned child, still nameless.

And what does he call his child? He calls it 'her baby'. Tucky's baby.

This is the final, and presumably unintentional, betrayal in Xavier Herbert's great novel about deserting fathers and abandoned children.

The Dead Do Not Die

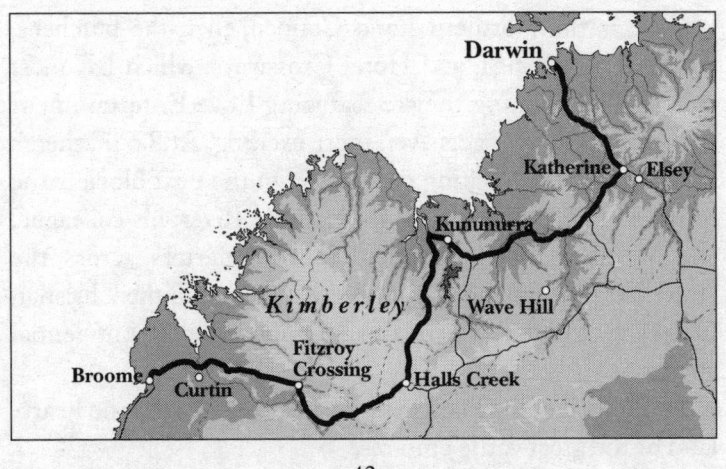

After a holiday week in beautiful, modern Darwin, which the cyclones keep permanently fresh and newly built, I long to get back to the dust and emptiness of the interior.

I drive south and stay overnight in Katherine, a small town with a population of ten thousand, an important crossroads with a bank, a post office, a police station and a main street crammed with the usual inland amusements.

There's Popeye's Pizza and the Bucking Bill Burger Bar Tasty Takeaways. 'Come in and see Aboriginal artists at work.' Cheek by jowl with Newton's saddlemakers is Jen's

Place, the fashion boutique. EVERYTHING MUST GO. The florist offers a wide selection of artificial flowers; the felt hats at the hatmaker's are guaranteed genuine and The Beauty Factory gives professional massages and beauty therapy. The southern end is shared by the newsagent and estate agent. No prices in the window.

If you cross the street and turn back north, the first thing you see is the Northern Land Council, then the butcher's, which also sells fish, and Hotel Crossways, which has most things. This evening they're featuring Love Entertainment & Co. On Friday it gets even more exciting. At 8 p.m. there's a show with 'toe-sucking cowgirls'. On the next block is the office of Tim Baldwin, MP for Victoria River; his colleague, the Member for Katherine, has his quarters across the street. Anyone still not satisfied can continue to the Christian Outreach Center, which this evening offers 'confidential advice'.

I go to bed early. The next morning, I drive into the heartland of the great cattle empires.

44

The Victoria Highway between Katherine and Kununurra runs through former Vestey property, which occupied something over a hundred thousand square kilometres of Northern Territory. That's more than three times the size of Belgium.

The jewel in the crown was Wave Hill Station.[76] The land was taken from the Gurindji and other Aboriginal peoples at the end of the nineteenth century. The peoples, or what was left of them, stayed where they were. They could not leave their holy places and the land that it was their traditional task to tend. They had to stay, but to be able to do so they had to work for the new owner, Vesteys. Their wages reflected the situation. In practice, northern Australia's meat production was achieved by use of a native labour force whose pay consisted of the right to remain on the land that had been stolen from them.

The racial divisions were acute and insurmountable. But in the mid-1960s, word spread of the black unrest in the USA. The American civil-rights movement sprouted offshoots in Australia. The North Australian Workers Union began organizing black workers and the Council for Aboriginal Rights formulated a programme with the following main points:

- Equal pay for equal work
- Social insurance payments to go not to the employer but direct to the worker
- Living accommodation for Aborigines to meet the same standards as that for whites
- Aborigines to be treated with as much respect as whites. Offensive racist expressions such as 'nigger' not allowed.

The press published pictures of ramshackle workers' accommodation at Wave Hill. The company replied that the pictures were not representative – all their other accommodation was better than this particular example. The press published profit figures and claimed the company could afford to pay black people the same wage as white people. The company at first answered that it paid low wages out of consideration for the

Aborigines, who did not know how to handle money. When this argument was scoffed at by the papers, the company maintained that the difference in wages was a competence issue. But it proved difficult to explain why every white worker, without exception, had displayed greater competence than every single black worker.

'For eighty-five years our people have accepted these conditions and worse, but on August 22, 1966, the Gurindji tribe decided to cease to live like dogs . . .' said Vincent Lingiari, and led the black workers and their families in a 'walk-out' from Wave Hill to Wattie Creek. It became one of the most famous strikes in Australian history. Initially, the focus was on the question of equal pay. But the underlying issue of land rights soon surfaced. In April 1967, the Gurindji people wrote to the Governor-General and demanded back a small part of the land that had been taken from them. They declared themselves willing to pay the same annual fee that Vesteys had paid up to that point. If Vesteys demanded compensation for handing over the land, the fifty years and more that the Aborigines had worked unpaid or for derisory wages should be considered compensation enough.

The Legislative Assembly set up a committee, which declared: 'There are strong moral arguments to support this people's demand for the restoration to them of a small share of the much larger area which they have regarded as their own since time immemorial.'

In August 1975, the Labor prime minister took part in a ceremony at Wattie Creek in which the right of ownership to 3,200 square kilometres of land was returned to the Gurindji people. It was celebrated as a famous victory. But 96.8 per cent of the problem remained. The battle for land had only just begun.

Victoria Highway runs along the boundary between wetlands and dry areas. A distinctive feature on the dry side is the spinifex, a sort of grass spear the height of a man, emerging point outward from a clump at the base. Armed grasses that know how to defend themselves, resined grasses that burn well, especially in the wet.

Another characteristic of the dry side is the trees' habit of shutting down some of their foliage during the winter season. Just as we lived in the warm, fragrant kitchen in the wartime winters of my childhood, keeping the living room closed off to save fuel, or as the farming communities of my childhood kept their best parlours shut and unheated until guests arrived, so

The boab tree. Illustration from J. Lort Stokes' *Discoveries in Australia* (1846).

these trees let half their foliage stand withered and deactivated over the winter, while their other half stays green.

The most distinctive vegetation on the wet side is the boab tree, which in Africa is known as the baobab. Looks like a bundle of branches stuck into a thick thermos flask. These trees are quite often hollow, their trunks roomy enough to be used as places of detention, as in Timber Creek, where I lunch in the shade of the former police station, which is now a museum.

Kununurra with its population of five thousand is a modern, fully planned, single-storey development, important for fruit-growing and sugar-cane production. Middle-class bungalows and shopping centres, administrative buildings, services, a country club and a tourist office – all of the latest design. The face Western Australia likes to show to the world. I have bed and breakfast at Duncan House, a trim little *pension*.

46

In my dream, I'm still staying at Duncan House. The years are passing. I'm taking it easy. There's nothing to do but wait in the permanently blowing wind. A tall young woman asks to borrow my bicycle. I'd forgotten that I had one. But her muscular back is impressive. Her vertebral column is magnificently flexible. Her backbone makes a dark runnel in her flesh. She swings herself up on to the bicycle and disappears. I stay sitting there, so impensioned that the newspaper bursts into flames in my hands. A tongue of fire licks upwards, the news instantly blackens and is borne away on the wind in great flakes.

From Kununurra it's twenty kilometres or so to the Great Northern Highway, which runs south across a wonderful white tableland – silver white, grey white, creamy white, blue white, dry white, green white, white white – always against a background of red soil punctuated by the occasional black-green tree.

Three hundred and forty kilometres later I reach Halls Creek, an old gold-digging town where cattle transport routes converge before going on east towards the Tanami Desert. There are double-decker road trains parked everywhere, loaded with cattle and engulfed in dense swarms of flies.

This was how Vesteys decided to invest its way out of the problem when it could no longer keep its black workforce in serfdom. Anthropologists Catherine and Ronald Berndt proposed investment in modern worker accommodation, day nurseries, maternity care and child allowances. The landowners opted instead to put their money into running the cattle station with helicopters, and transport by means of road trains. Their former stockmen now swell the ranks of the unemployed in all the small settlements edging the Great Sandy Desert.

After Halls Creek there are long, straight sections; great stretches with evidence of fire damage; and numerous dead kangaroos at the roadside, traffic-accident victims, with birds of prey hovering above them. Now and then a hill, surrounded by material from landslides. Occasional turnings to solitary stations, like in Patagonia.

On the main highway, absolutely nothing happens for 290 kilometres.

Fitzroy Crossing is a newly built, well-designed town a short distance from the ruins of the old one. In the big supermarket and shopping centre, black people predominate. The Fitzroy Lodge Hotel is raised on pillars, with parking places below and a swimming pool in the middle. I sit writing on the loggia outside my room in the cool of the sunset. A few insects. A swell of rowdy, inebriated voices from the hotel's all-white bar. I glimpse the occasional woman, but mostly I see nothing but men in hats. They have become virtually unthinkable without hats. Do they make love in their hats? Do they even take them off to go to sleep?

Most of them are well and truly drunk, and don't come weaving up to their rooms until three in the morning when the bar closes. The female occupant of the room next to mine turns in with a crash. Just before seven the next morning, she starts her car and drives away, heavily made-up to hide the ravages of the previous night, but still alive.

48

North of the Great Northern Highway lies Kimberley, wooded and hilly. A remarkable chapter in the history of Swedish scholarship was played out here, the 'Swedish Expedition to Australia 1910–11', led by the zoologist Eric Mjöberg (1882–1938). The planned activities of the expedition were to include 'an attempt to bring back as many skeletons as possible of the interesting Australian negro race, which is increasingly dying out'.

The Swedish expedition seems oblivious to the scientific debate of the time about Aboriginal social systems. The only thing of interest to Mjöberg is their skeletons.

Zoologist and grave robber Eric Mjöberg (1882–1938).

Collecting these was a delicate undertaking involving considerable inconvenience and difficulty, according to Mjöberg. 'Nothing is so risky as stealing people's dead from them.' On New Year's Day 1911, he succeeds nonetheless in 'snatching an exquisitely well preserved skeleton which in accordance with local custom had been laid to rest on a bed of eucalyptus logs up in the crown of a eucalyptus. But only a few days later the negroes tracked me down, and news spread like wildfire all over the district that I had desecrated their dead.'

Thus runs Mjöberg's preliminary report in the scientific journal *Ymer* of 1912. In his more popularly written travelogue *Bland vilda djur och folk i Australien* (Among Wild Animals and Peoples in Australia, 1915), he describes 'the Australian aboriginal' with thinly concealed distaste: 'His nose is broad, flat, repulsively ugly, his nostrils wide, the root of the nose somehow pushed inwards. His eyes are deep-set, bloodshot, his look sly and shifty.'[77]

In the chapter entitled 'Hunting for the Bones of the Dead', he relates the episode of the dead body in the crown of the tree:

I climbed up into the tree and found I had a good view of the deathbed. The smell was in truth anything but pleasant.

Safely back on the ground, I did a quick tally [of the bones] and found that they were all there, with the exception of one little bone from the base of the hand.

This was the first anthropological material and a splendid acquisition for my collection.

On the way home, Mjöberg passes a burial place called Skeleton Hill and finds a number of dead bodies in a cave. 'I managed to extract two lovely skulls. The bottom jaws were missing, however, and I only located them after a long search.'

'In the depths of the dark caves, generations of aboriginals lay buried. No white man had ever before disturbed the peace of the natural grave vaults.'

'Pleased and tired, I set off on my homeward journey . . .'

He has hidden the bones in sacks. His companions are worried that the 'negroes' will realize what is in the sacks, but Mjöberg tricks the Aborigines into believing they are just kangaroo bones. 'I was laughing inside as the three niggers walked ahead of me in cheerful conversation, carrying the remains of their dead comrades.'[78]

49

The Aborigines warn him not to desecrate any more graves. They 'express their indignation at my activities', Mjöberg writes. In his capacity as a scientist he realizes that their view of the dead is linked to religious ideas, but sees no need to respect these. 'It was only to be expected that these ideas and feelings would be deeply rooted amongst a people by no means liberated from the dark reaches of suspicion, superstition and primitive notions.'

So when a young man dies of fever, Mjöberg sees his chance and asks to attend the burial. His request is refused. Mjöberg however follows the funeral procession at a distance. 'They were clearly suspicious of my presence. But I for my part was firmly resolved not to let such an exceptional opportunity slip through my fingers.'[79]

In view of the 'negro's' nature, as he saw it, Mjöberg was thereby exposing himself to great personal risk: 'A negro never kills in an open or honest combat. No, that is too much at odds with his wily, treacherous nature. It is the ambush that is his strength and his weapon. And when he kills, he kills unerringly.'

From a distance, Mjöberg observes the dead man being laid to rest in a tree. 'What a splendid opportunity for me after a while to retrieve Sambo from his airy bier and add his bones to my collection, I thought to myself.'

What he is planning 'was in the eyes of the blacks a grave crime'. They can guess his intentions, and when he comes to fetch the skeleton, he finds the grave empty. 'Evidently rumour and suspicion had conspired to upset my plans. In future skeleton hunts I would need to exercise even greater caution, for the Australian negro is very unreliable, and highly fanatical in all his superstition.'

At Cherubin's cattle station in Kimberley, Mjöberg meets a young 'negro', whom he 'cultivates with all the means at my disposal' until he reveals where the dead of the area are buried. 'He was a cheaply bought Judas Iscariot.'[80]

'Despite all my precautions, it had leaked out that I was hunting the dead, and groups of negroes gathered round the station with grim and threatening expressions.' They had also as a precaution taken the bodies of their dead and hidden them.

Mjöberg is on the verge of giving up when his companion points to a hollow eucalyptus tree. 'I stuck in my hand and it came up against a skeleton, semi-decayed and still in one piece.'

At this point his helper refuses all further involvement. 'Single-handedly I had to work loose the individual parts, so they could be packed in the smaller sacks I had brought with me.

'With this, I was able to add another valuable skeleton to my collection.'

Mjöberg knew that 'there is a strict law forbidding all export from Australia of the Australian negroes, skeletons or parts of them'. But he considered that as a scientist he was above the law, and describes with pride his conscious breaking of it. Altogether he triumphantly took home six skeletons and some skulls, which were added to the collections of the Stockholm Ethnographical Museum – where they lay untouched for ninety years, while scholarship went in other directions.

After a debate in the national daily *Dagens Nyheter* in the autumn of 2003, Sweden declared its willingness to return the skeletons stolen by Mjöberg. State museums were required to carry out inventories of all the human remains in their possession and offer to return them to any surviving descendants.

50

The Great Northern Highway continues along the fringes of the Great Sandy Desert, but not much of it is to be seen – the landscape is so flat that the smallest bush obscures the view. The only things offering any variety are the flares of burning grass and bushes, and the birds of prey circling above the flames, waiting to hunt down small animals as they flee.

On the road into Derby there's a thousand-year-old prison tree, as big as the Runde Taarn tower in Copenhagen. It's a boab with a diameter of fourteen metres, which was used to detain Aboriginal prisoners on their way to the police jail in Derby. The jail, too, is now a historic monument, open to visitors. That's what you find in town after town. In both Sweden and the USA I've seen former prisons converted into hotels, but Australians in these remote parts seem sold on prisons and police stations as signposts to the past. Not schools, nor churches, nor bridges and other constructions – but specifically jails. Maybe a fixation from Australia's time as a penal colony? Maybe it's the infrastructure of state violence that best represents history in this part of the country?

Forty kilometres from Derby at Curtin lies the Australian Air Force base which from 1999 to 2002 was also a so-called detention centre – that is, an internment camp – for 1,400 asylum seekers from Afghanistan, Iran and Iraq. The camp was run by a private company, Australasian Corrective Services (ACS), which on paper was under the control of the Immigration Department. In practice, treatment of the inmates was left entirely to the company.[81]

The internees were kept first in tents, then in sheet-metal barracks. All accommodation was subject to searches and reallocation at any time of day or night. Contact with the world outside was strictly rationed. Hundreds of internees had to share one newspaper and one television set. Any articles critical of Curtin would have been cut out of the newspaper in advance.

Visitors had to apply in advance in writing for permission to visit a given prisoner, and include written evidence that the prisoner himself had initiated contact and asked for the visit. Of three hundred telephone lines, only six payphones could be used by the 1,400 internees. Incoming calls had to be approved in advance by both the Department and the camp authorities. If you weren't on the list, your call wasn't connected.

Even faxes were blocked, if they weren't from the Department or a legal representative – something most of the asylum seekers lacked. All faxes from families, lovers, friends and other prohibited contacts were immediately shredded. In many cases, this destroyed crucial evidence in the asylum seekers' cases.

The first hunger strike came five months after the opening of the camp, and lasted for nine days. The next hunger strike lasted twenty-six days before it was violently crushed. Suicide and attempted suicide became increasingly common.

'The Freedom Bus' was the name given to an activist initiative to provide legal help to the asylum seekers. The bus travelled round Australia in 2002, visiting all the internment camps. After protracted correspondence, the lawyers were half promised a visit to Curtin. The day of the planned visit arrived. The activists had to walk five kilometres in searing heat. Reaching the fence, they were informed that the only personnel able to take decisions were 'out fishing'. Permission to visit was categorically refused.

Two days later, two women from the Freedom Bus were allowed a two-hour meeting with five internees at an abandoned airstrip fifteen kilometres from the camp. The camp staff seized their gifts and documents, claiming that these would be kept safe and, subject to approval by the camp management, given to the internees if and when they were released.

The visit was supervised and videoed by the camp staff. The internees spoke in whispers, with frantic intensity. Four of the five were on hunger strike, along with two hundred other internees. Desperately they tried to explain their plight in a language they could barely speak. Requests for interpreters were not granted. Nor were the internees permitted to hand over the forty-page document they had prepared about conditions in the camp.

Soon after this, the desperate asylum seekers set fire to the camp. It was closed in September 2002 and the last internees were transferred to other camps or to the prison at Broome.

51

Broome is the pearl of the west coast, in more than one sense. It was pearls that created the town and made it as rich and pleasant as it is today.

It all started with black boys diving for mussels in the bays along the coast. Sometimes they found pearls, which white men happily took in exchange for a little tobacco or an old penknife. Later, companies were formed, which 'employed' native divers. 'A sack of flour and a hank of tobacco bought a human life.' The cattle-station owners got £5 for every boy they hired out, and did good business. Agents rounded up boys from way out in the desert, boys who had never seen the sea. They were lassoed and dragged after the horses if they refused to come voluntarily.

The boys were taken to the island of Lacepedes north of Broome. No one there cared how they had been hired. 'One nigger was as black as another.' They all signed with a cross the contract that in practice became their death warrant.

After the contract ceremony, the boys were taken to the ships, and sent out in small boats at dawn, one white man to eight to ten naked boy divers. One after another they climbed over the rail, turned in the water and swam to the seabed. Ten metres was the norm but sometimes they were forced to dive as deep as eighteen metres. They were down there for thirty seconds to a minute. Then the shining heads broke the surface and the mussels were thrown into the boat. A few minutes' breathing space, then came a rap on the knuckles with the oar: down again! If they lost a boy, there were always plenty more to replace him. Most of them didn't even last two years as divers. Those who survived were often lame or invalids by the time they were put ashore to make their way home as best they could.[82]

In the Protector's view, six was a suitable age for a black boy to be hired out as a pearl fisher. If he managed to run away, he would be brought back to his employer by the police.

It took harsh discipline for a single white man to be able to force ten Aboriginal boys to do deadly dangerous work they loathed. The divers were forbidden to talk to one another in the boats; they could only reply to the white man's questions. The whole day could pass without a word being uttered. If anyone refused, two experienced divers would grab him tightly by the wrists and swim to the bottom holding him between them. After that brutal initiation, no one made a fuss again.

The trick was to stay down long enough to gather enough mussels, but not too long. The instant a diver can no longer hold his breath, his upward motion is arrested and his body starts slowly sinking. Quick action from his comrades could sometimes save him, but many divers never came back up. Even the most experienced were risking their lives with every dive.

The local bishop reported boys whose hands had been smashed on the boat's rail because they were taking too long between dives, and children who were whipped and left to die on the beach when the bends had rendered them useless.[83]

There was no question of wages. The blacks 'didn't under-stand money', the boat owners said. A shirt and a pair of trousers at the start of the season, food and tobacco while they were working – this was the usual remuneration. Rumours spread about what it was like on the boats, and boys had to be taken from deeper and deeper in the desert, and with ever rougher methods. Firearms, ox whips and neck-irons became standard items of equipment for the agents recruiting 'volun-teers' to the pearl boats.

In the town museum, it is only fitting that the pearl has pride of place. But there they let the story begin around 1900, when the industry starts employing highly specialized, highly paid Japanese and Malayan divers with modern technical equipment. Not a word about the black boy divers.

52

I and my cousin was at the post office with my Mum and Auntie. They put us into the police ute [a small flatbed truck] and said they were taking us to Broome. They put the mums in there as well. But when we'd gone about ten miles they stopped and threw the mothers out of the car. We jumped on our mothers' backs, crying, trying not to be left behind. But the policemen pulled us off and threw us back in the car. They pushed the mothers away and drew off, while our mothers were chasing the car. When we got to Broome they put me and my cousin in the Broome lock-up. We were only ten years old. We were in the lock-up two days waiting for the boat to Perth.[84]

This happened in 1935, by which time the police had already been abducting children for over twenty years. Black boys were no longer being kidnapped into slavery on the pearl boats; instead, the fairer-skinned 'half-bloods' were being kidnapped and taken to institutions where they were brought up as cheap labour, as farmhands or maids for the whites. The justification for this, here as in the Northern Territory, was the need to make the most of the supposedly superior 'white' gene pool among the mixed-race children, to lift them out of the black slums and assimilate them into white society.

The children were taught to despise their own language and culture. All ties with parents, relatives and friends were severed. They were even separated from their brothers and sisters. If two children from the same family happened to be placed in the same institution or white family, the fact that they were siblings was denied. Many have testified to discovering only later that they were sharing a 'home' with their brother or sister.

53

I spend a few days in pleasant Broome. Visit the pioneering Aboriginal publishing house Magabala Books. Make purchases in the well-stocked bookshop. Eat at Matsos Café & Store where the deep veranda offers shade and catches the wind. Stay at the Mangrove Hotel, from whose windows, evening after evening, I see the bush fires glowing on the other side of the mangrove swamp.

The Great Northern Highway running south looks on the map as if it's squeezed between the desert and the sea with a

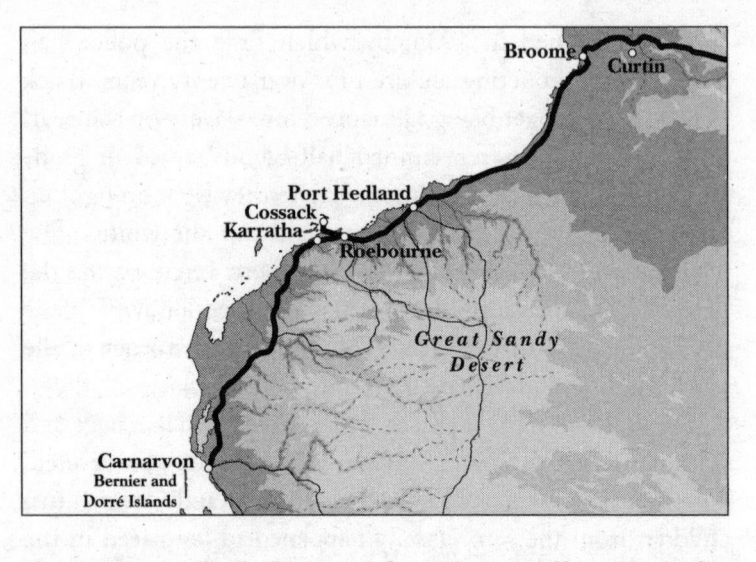

clear view over both. In actual fact, it starts off so utterly flat that you see nothing but thicket and brush, brush and thicket. For almost four hundred kilometres, it's like the littered remnants of a forest after a gigantic clear felling project.

No other part of Australia has given me such a powerful sense of no-man's-land. There are no roads leading out into the desert, no roads leading down to the sea; nothing happens along the road except the grubby and dilapidated little Sandfire Roadhouse, totally free of any redeeming features. There's a turning down to an equally charmless campsite by the beach, from which you are grateful to return to the main highway.

And then it happens. After four hundred kilometres, the landscape suddenly opens out, the undergrowth disappears and a magnificent, majestic monotony takes its place. Endless kilometres between hedges of yellow mimosa. Endless kilometres across plains of dry, sparkling white grass. And way off in the distance, right on the horizon, a caravan of mountains looking like humpy camels.

It's the flatness that can make you think of Australia as ugly and empty. The flatness keeps you captive in the bushes. But as soon as the road rises a little and lets you see over the top of the thicket, fantastical landscapes are revealed. White salt lakes rimmed with red foam and beaches of red sand. Round. Meandering. Long and narrow. Luminous. Dry lakes where the salt is all that is left of the fresh water. Lakes that grow, spread out, form whole land-scapes of white veils, of pink patches, of long stripes.

Australia is *striped*. My whole field of vision is filled with *lines*. Left by water that once ran there? Or did the wind draw them in the sand?

Grooves. Scratches. Clawmarks. Like those torn by the inland ice into the flat rock surfaces of Sweden. All in the same direction. In this divine monotony, it looks just as though an army of pastry wheels has advanced across thinly rolled, light red biscuit dough.

54

Nearer Port Hedland, the salt lakes of the desert give way to artificial salt lagoons producing one of the town's most impor-tant exports. The west coast of Australia exports salt, meat and iron ore on a large scale through Port Hedland docks. The townscape is dominated by cranes and huge conveyors. The town itself is only two or three streets across, and situated on a peninsula surrounded by tidal mudflats. I check into the Mercure Inn and lie there listening to the hum and buzz. Ten thousand kilometres separate me from Woomera, where I heard the sparrows taking a dustbath. I've reached the other end of the world's biggest firing range.

'The library? It's opposite the detention centre,' the lady says, just as anyone else might say, 'It's opposite the cathedral,' or 'opposite the town hall'. The internment camp is the natural point from which people take their bearings here.

'What's a detention centre?' I ask with all the innocence of a foreigner.

'The House of Correction,' she replies in surprise. (And I read in her face the inaudibly added remark: 'Don't you know *anything*, thickhead?') 'Though it's the boat people they keep there these days.'

It was my first prison of the day. Then I got to Roebourne. And where was the tourist information office if not in 'the Old Gaol', now a museum? I went on to Cossack, where they serve sandwiches in The Old Tollhouse, now a café. And what was there to see in the place? The Old Gaol, of course. A stone building with three cells and barred windows. The rest of the town has gone; only the street names are left, clearly marked by street signs in the vast emptiness.

Everyone knows that eastern Australia was historically a place to which British convicts were deported. But even here on the west coast, which was never a penal colony, the prisons are the only permanent features to survive, the only things stable enough to weather all the storms. Even on this coast, there's a strong sense of Australia as a penal culture.

55

On 28 September 1983, sixteen-year-old John Pat was taken into custody after a clash between Aborigines and police at the Hotel Victoria in Roebourne. He died in a police cell the same night.

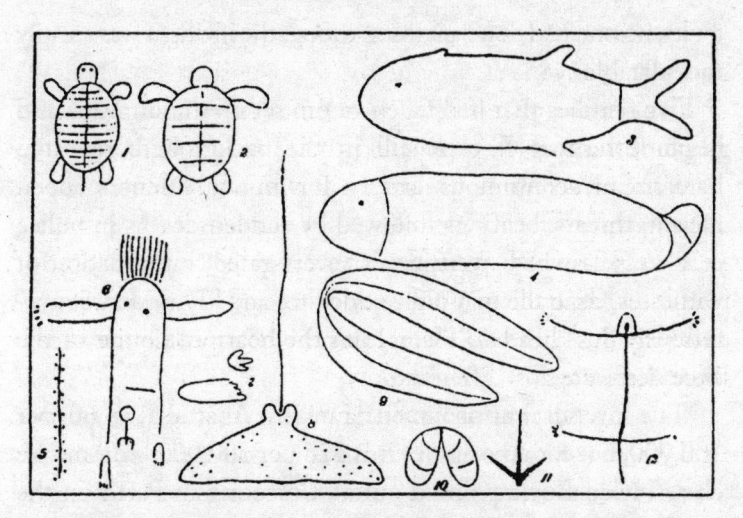

Rock carvings from Port Hedland. Illustration from Herbert Basedow's *The Australian Aboriginal* (1925).

Roebourne is an old port town with ingrained racial antagonism, particularly between white police officers and black youths. In the words of one district judge who regularly presides over court proceedings in Roebourne, the police terrorize the town's Aborigines. 'This is a town on the boil,' he added.[85]

When no explanation was given for the sudden death of a healthy young man, tensions boiled over. On 7 October, some hundred black people, chanting 'Murderers, murderers,' attacked the Hotel Victoria, vandalized the restaurant and emptied the bar of strong liquor.

To calm the mood, a police investigation of the death was launched. Five officers were accused of manslaughter but released in 1984. The family thought it could see a pattern. All too often, apparently healthy young men died without warning after being taken into police custody. No one was guilty, no one had done anything wrong; the incident was simply inexplicable.

Five families that had fallen victim set up a committee and began collecting facts to fill in the background: repeated harassment, continuous arrests for minor offences, open racism, threats, beatings followed by sudden deaths in police cells or jails which were never investigated, intimidation of witnesses, contradictory police evidence and key evidence mysteriously 'lost'. In two cases, even the heart and brain of the deceased were 'lost' after autopsy.

'The overall imprisonment rate in Australia is 60 per 100,000, but for Aborigines it is 726 per 100,000,' committee chair Helen Boyle pointed out at a meeting in Perth on the third anniversary of John Pat's death. A black person is twelve times more likely to be arrested and convicted than a white person. And the risk of dying in custody is many times higher if you are black.

Five years after John Pat's death, a wide-ranging inquiry was set up, and the resulting report, 'Black Deaths in Custody', raised national awareness of the problem of racist police violence. The Victoria Hotel in Roebourne is still there. The pub's worth a visit but there's no temptation to stay overnight.

56

Today, the sky has been the dominant feature. The ground has just been a short little strip at my feet – the rest has been sky. I recall my disappointment when I bought my first camera and started taking pictures; I found that all those glorious views consisted of nothing but a thin line of ground under an immense curtain of sky. I lost faith in photography, gave my camera away.

Giralia is a station that offers bed and breakfast on the long, empty stretch between Karratha and Carnarvon. The accommodation consists of four portable metal huts with WC and shower. Three of them are divided into five cabins with two bunks in each. There's just enough room to put your feet on the floor between the bunks, and just enough room for your bag between the end of the bunk and the short wall. Electric power is provided by a diesel motor that stops its noisy chugging about nine at night, and then by batteries charged by solar energy during the day. A well for water and its own private water tower. The whole station is being rebuilt after the last cyclone. It had twenty-five thousand sheep before natural disaster struck, and now has eighteen thousand.

There's nobody staying in the cabins around me, except for a road scraper called Tom and his wife. He moves from station to station and scrapes their roads for them. It turns out we were born in the same year, so Tom greets me effusively, lets me see his index finger with its top joint missing, shows off his flat stomach and abundant hair, and shares with me his rich experience of life as a cattle herder, truck driver and road scraper. He's got a small property up north, where he's thinking of going to live in a few years. But he can't imagine stopping work. Work keeps your stomach flat, your hair long, and old age at bay. Work is an insurance policy against death. From the proposition 'If you're working you're not dead,' it's just one short step to 'If you're working you won't die.'

Dinner consists of vegetable soup, chicken out of a packet and crème caramel. For breakfast next morning, we each get a big sausage with scrambled egg. In the meantime it's night, dark, clear and starry. The moon lies splashing in its bathtub. The Milky Way is a vastness of scrambled stars, really a mush of stars covering virtually the whole sky. A small horse and a few solitary sheep are grazing near the buildings. I sink like a stone into sleep.

57

In my dream I see the sea, the utterly calm sea.

I see the coast, the utterly still coast.

When this utterly calm sea meets this utterly still coast, huge breakers are suddenly thrown up.

Two sorts of stillness touch one another and explode in roars and foam.

58

Off the town of Carnarvon lie two long, narrow, red sandstone islands called Bernier and Dorré. The Dutch explorer William de Vlamingh came here in 1696 and found that there was no water on the islands. The British explorer George Grey came here in February 1839 and was forced to drink rainwater which his men sucked out of the sandstone and spat into a pail. There wasn't a tree or a blade of grass. The fauna was predominantly mosquitoes and rats. A cyclone tore across the islands with such force that grown men were knocked down like children. After the hurricane, all the supplies were contaminated by seawater, the ammunition was damaged, the clocks no longer worked and the boats seemed impossible to repair.[86]

At the start of the twentieth century, these two islands were selected for the forcible internment and treatment of Aborigines suffering from sexually transmitted diseases, above all syphilis. This illness was unheard of before the whites arrived, and the infection was spread mainly by male white settlers chasing after black women, but it was considered more appropriate to intern the natives, especially women, in order to reduce the risk of infection for white men.[87]

The proposal was put forward in 1903 by the Aborigines' Protector in Western Australia. He claimed coercive measures needed to be taken against the Aboriginal women to prevent them 'pandering to the lusts of Asiatics, who are so numerous and ubiquitous'. So the blame was put on the women and the Chinese, but the proposed measures were intended to protect the very people who were the primary source of the illness: the white men.

In the villages of the outback, it was the police who made the diagnoses and decided which of the indigenous people needed treatment. The police lined up the men and above all the women, and inspected their sexual organs. Those who were considered sick were treated as criminals and held captive in neck-irons during long marches through the desert. The number of arrests was determined by the number of neck-irons available on the chain. They were marched from place to place until all the neck-irons were taken. It was not unusual for women in neck-irons to be raped by the police or fellow prisoners. Those who weren't sick when they were seized fell ill on the march.

The police were in no great hurry to deliver the patients they had rounded up to the hospital. Some of those taken prisoner because of sickness remained in chains for three years, carrying out hard physical labour in tropical heat. As late as 1958, the police of Western Australia were defending use of neck-irons by claiming the natives preferred them.

A large proportion of the costs to the state of Aboriginal welfare went on salaries for a doctor and a couple of nurses for several hundred black patients on the two islands. The first of them arrived in October 1908. The method of treating sexually transmitted diseases at that time involved painful injections and operations, usually ineffectual. Experiments were carried out on the patients; they were given a series of different injections, some of which probably killed more than they cured. The majority of those taken to the islands never returned.

Framboesia, from the French word for raspberry, is a tropical skin disease which occurs and spreads particularly among undernourished children living in conditions of primitive hygiene. Spongy, raspberry-like growths decompose, leaving sores. In 1914, a new doctor found that most of the patients on Bernier and Dorré were suffering not from syphilis but from framboesia. The diagnosis had been wrong, the treatment misdirected, the internment unnecessary, and the alleged threat to the white population far less than had been feared. Financial support was cut drastically, and by 1918 there was nothing left on 'the Islands of the Dead' but the graves of all the patients who had died during treatment.

All the great men of ideas who between 1910 and 1913 were seeking the answer to the puzzle of the birth of mankind among the indigenous peoples of Australia had one thing in common: none of them had been to Australia. Morgan and Engels, Frazer and Freud, Kropotkin, Durkheim and Malinowski all happily discussed the Aborigines' way of life without themselves ever having seen an Aborigine.

The young postgraduate student Malinowski did at least realize this was a problem, which he tried to solve by means of a rigourously critical approach to sources. His professor, William Rivers, had a background in the experimental sciences and wanted to go still further. The study of the original inhabitants of the world had always been an 'amateur science', he maintained, and would remain so for as long as it was dependent on chance observations by explorers and missionaries. Scholars should make personal contact with the natives, and confine themselves to studying their family relationships, because the extended family provided the basis for their whole social life.

The main advantage of the 'genealogical method', as Rivers called it, was that it was self-checking: incorrect information would easily be identified, because it would soon be contradicted by information from other family members. This methodology would make ethnology the only branch of social sciences able to achieve results with a scientific precision to match that of the natural sciences, Rivers declared in his lectures in 1910.

Rivers was an inspiration to a young man called Alfred Brown, who would later become famous under the name

Radcliffe-Brown. He travelled to Western Australia, equipped an expedition, set off inland, and near the small town of Sandstone found an Aboriginal encampment where he began his genealogical research.

The peace was soon shattered by the police, who one night surrounded the camp and rode to and fro, trampling huts and campfires, shooting their weapons in the air and shouting orders to the natives to line up for inspection. A murder that had taken place many hundreds of kilometres away was used as an excuse for terrorizing Aborigines all over the state. While they were at it, they took the opportunity of inspecting the women's sexual organs and taking some of them away to Sandstone, where other unfortunates were waiting to begin the long march to forcible treatment on the islands.[88]

The police action destroyed any chance of success for Radcliffe-Brown's work in Sandstone. He decided to go to the islands instead, where he would be able to question the natives in peace, without any police disturbance. And no one would be able to sneak off to avoid being questioned. The scene was set for the first experiment to employ the genealogical method.

60

Radcliffe-Brown concentrated on terms for expressing relationship in the Kareira people, which at the time of the whites' arrival appear to have comprised some seven hundred individuals, of whom about a hundred were left by 1911.[89] They were linked together by a complicated system of family relationships, as can be seen from the following mini-dictionary:

Maeli Paternal grandfather, paternal grandfather's brothers, maternal grandmother's brother, spouse's maternal grandfather and (if the speaker is a man) son's son and son's daughter.

Kabali Paternal grandmother, paternal grandmother's sisters, spouse's maternal grandmother and (if the speaker is a woman) son's son and son's daughter.

Mama Father, paternal uncle, maternal aunt's husband and spouse's maternal uncle.

Nganga Mother, maternal aunt, paternal uncle's wife and spouse's paternal aunt.

Kaga Maternal uncle, paternal aunt's wife and father-in-law.

Nuba If the speaker is a man: my wife, my maternal uncles' daughters, my paternal aunts' daughters, my brothers' wives and my wife's sisters. If the speaker is a woman: my husband, my maternal uncles' sons, my paternal aunts' sons, my sisters' husbands and my husband's brothers.

This little lexicon only includes the most important terms and their primary meanings. The term *mama*, father, is for example also used for all those my father calls brothers, as well as my maternal uncles' wives' brothers and the maternal uncles of my brothers-in-law. The list of who has the right to be called *mama* can be extended almost *ad infinitum*. But ask a man: Who is your *mama*? and he will reply with the name of his father, or if applicable his foster-father, although there is a whole series of other people he also calls *mama*.

Thus, just like us, the Kareira people distinguish between close and distant relatives. But the distant relatives' position in the family network is of far greater significance for the Kareira. Their society consists in its entirety of more or less close or distant relatives. The Kareira address small children by name, everyone else is addressed in terms of the relationships – father, mother, grandfather, grandmother etc. As a member of the Kareira you cannot have social relations with anyone other than relatives, since it is the relationship between you that determines how you should behave towards each other, and other forms of intercourse do not exist. It is highly unusual for there to be no family connection whatsoever between two Aborigines, but if that is the case it implies a latent threat.

Spencer and Gillen, who studied the totem rites of the Arrernte people, found that their totemic relations were the basis of the tribe's social life. In Radcliffe-Brown's work, the totem system is peripheral. He studies family terms among the Kareira people and finds, not surprisingly, that 'The entire tribe's social life is determined by kinship.'

61

In his questioning of the island internees, Radcliffe-Brown used a fifty-year-old Irishwoman, Daisy Bates, as an intermediary. Much later, she wrote in her autobiography that the Islands of the Dead were the saddest thing she had experienced in all her long life with the indigenous people of Australia.[90]

She could never forget the anguish and despair in their faces. They were taken from their homeland without knowing why, or where they were going. After marches of many hundreds of kilometres in neck-irons, they were shipped in fragile little craft across the sea, which they had never seen before, to those desolate islands where no one but strangers awaited them.

They were frightened of the hospital, with its endless tests and injections; they were frightened of each other, both alive and dead; they were frightened of the sea and of the hurricanes that heaved the sea in over the islands. They were undernourished, as weeks could go by without essential supplies when stormy weather prevented ships from putting in. Many succumbed to mental illness and tried to walk on the water to return home, or sat for days on end pouring sand over their heads. Others cried night and day in an interminable monotony of grief. Even death offered no consolation since their souls, so far from home, would be among none but enemies.

Used to extremely close family ties, but cut off from all contact with their people, they would often stand in silence at the furthest point of the promontory, in the vain hope of catching a glimpse of a loved one somewhere out there, on the far shore.

To be forcibly moved and forcibly treated for alleged sexually transmitted diseases on a remote island in the ocean, bereft of all contact with family, relations and friends – that would have been bad enough if it had happened to you or me. For the Kareira, a people whose 'social life is determined by kinship', isolation on the islands was even more dreadful. But Radcliffe-Brown never drew that conclusion.

The newly introduced policy of taking fairer-skinned children into custody and sending them to what in my childhood were called 'reformatories' would have been cruel enough treatment for anyone. But abducting children from a people like the Kareira, for whom kinship plays such a crucial role, was dealing a fatal blow to the heart of their society. Radcliffe-Brown never drew that uncomfortable conclusion either.

When in 1913 he began reporting the results of his studies in the *Journal of the Royal Anthropological Institute*, he was somewhat reticent in his description of the concentration camps where he had collected his data. He wrote that they had been 'obtained during a journey through the country of the tribes referred to'. Full stop.

Radcliffe-Brown was alone among the scholars of 1913 in visiting Australia and meeting Aborigines. But there is nothing to indicate that he really saw them. Perhaps he was so obsessed with his 'genealogical method' that he failed to make the connection between the significance of family and the sufferings of the Aborigines around him. Perhaps he thought it undiplomatic from a career point of view even to hint at the connection?

Sure enough, Radcliffe-Brown became Australia's first professor in his subject. Daisy Bates, with equal logic, ended up in a tent in the desert where she spent the following twenty-five years as guardian angel to her black friends.

To Pinjarra

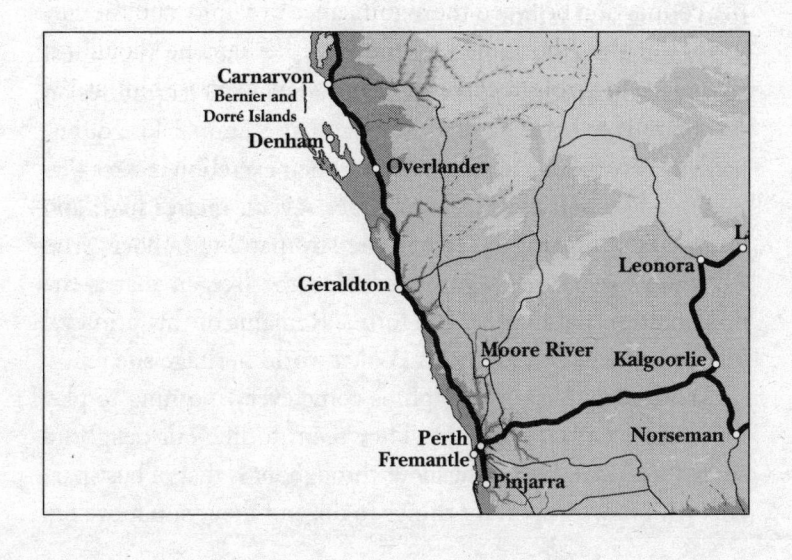

62

Another cool, sunny day. There's still water on the ground after yesterday's rain, throwing a sudden cascade of blue flowers along the verges. Fleshy leaves with claws along their veins; well-defended thorny stalks; the whole plant spangled with delicate, sky-blue flowers. It all has the air of an overnight improvisation, produced by the rain and already about to go to seed.

The ants bring sand to the surface and deposit it in red rings around their holes on the grey ground. The resulting landscape is as full of red spots as an Aboriginal painting.

After Overlander I swing out towards Denham. The beach is covered in pulverized shells. Little white shells, a few of them whole, but the majority crushed. The roads are long, straight and as dizzyingly beautiful as aerial photographs, the road rising and falling.

Hamelin Pool is known as the home of the world's largest colony of the world's oldest life form, single-celled creatures on the boundary between the plant and the animal kingdoms, halfway between algae and bacteria. Their excretion creates formations like tiered cakes, sometimes several metres high and known as stromatolites. It was the stromatolite builders who 3.5 billion years ago began producing the oxygen that is the precondition for all other life forms. Remains of this primeval life are protected in Hamelin Pool, a world heritage site.

At Monkey Mia, the dolphins come every morning to play for a while with us humans. They seem to like our delightful spontaneity, but their demeanour throughout is that of busy parents with more important things to do, and they soon move on.

63

Radcliffe-Brown and his disciples extended their mapping of Aboriginal family ties right across Australia. He summarized the results of his work with the genealogical method in *The Social Organization of the Australian Tribes* (1930–1).

The basis of traditional Aboriginal society is the family,

consisting of a man and one or more wives, plus their children. Two or more families constitute a 'horde', who together own and control a specific territory, where they hunt and gather. Most hordes belong to a 'clan', which carries out rites in holy places within the territory of the horde. In these rites, the participants reincarnate mythical ancestors and dramatize their feats.

Hordes that speak the same language form a 'tribe', or more correctly a 'people'. A people is unified by language and custom, but is not under the orders of any central leadership. Most peoples are divided into named halves, 'moieties', which in turn are usually also divided into halves. A man from one half must always take his wife from the other half, sub-half or sub-sub-half.

Every child is born into a complicated kinship system which is considered more important than both horde and people. Everybody knows how everybody is related to everybody else, and the rights and obligations this entails.

The underlying principle is that of sibling relationships. A man and his brothers are classed together, as are a woman and her sisters. Those we would call 'uncle', the Aborigine calls 'father'. Aunts are called 'mother'; cousins are called 'brother' or 'sister'.

Another basic principle is that those who marry into the family are treated like blood relations. The wife of every man I call 'father' I will call 'mother', although she did not give birth to me, and originally belonged to another family entirely. In the same way, the husband of a woman I call 'mother' will become my 'father'. Thus I may have many mothers and fathers, who in their turn may have many mothers and fathers, all of whom I call 'grandfather/grandmother' (on both the maternal and the paternal side).

The third principle is that there is no limit to the application of the two previous ones. They do not cease to apply beyond the horde or the people. Kinship crosses all boundaries, so every Aborigine is in some way related to every other. Which before the white invasion meant that every human being was in some way related to every other human being, and thereby had the right to be treated as 'father', 'mother' or some other close relative.[91]

Radcliffe-Brown presents these conclusions quite baldly, without a single word to indicate how he arrived at them. Occasionally he refers to his own, unpublished notes of 1911–12, but he never describes a concrete situation.

Nor is there any concrete reference to the rights and obligations that family kinship implies. Which were the problems the family system was designed to overcome? Was it perhaps at heart a pension system? Might it have been a way of organizing childcare or distributing welfare benefits? It is, after all, inherent in the system that the relationships of the close family, of one's own home, are metaphorically extended to the whole family, the whole nation, in fact to every fellow man or woman. Wasn't it in fact a family-based but unlimited welfare state, uniting family members across all boundaries, that the Aborigines were trying to create in the deserts of Australia?

64

Mary Montgomerie Bennett's father, Robert Christison, owned a vast sheep station, but the sheep had a mysterious tendency to disappear.[92] One day when he was out looking for missing sheep, he caught sight of four Aborigines carrying something heavy between them in a kangaroo skin. What was it? Believing he had caught a gang of sheep stealers red-handed, he galloped at full speed towards the Aborigines, who set down their burden and ran.

When the skin was opened, he found to his amazement not a dead sheep but a human being: a very old, severely handicapped woman. Her hair was white, her teeth worn right down. But she appeared well nourished and cared for. She was so terrified that she could not utter a word. The black farmhands recognized her, however, explaining that she had been crippled from birth and that members of her family took it in turns to carry her as they covered long distances on foot.

The incident gave Christison food for thought. For his daughter Mary, it was life-changing. Everything she had ever been told about brute savages and childishly irresponsible natives was turned on its head. She realized with astonishment that the blacks would not think of abandoning one another, but took responsibility even for the most helpless and vulnerable members of their family. It was brought home to her with all the force of a bolt of lightning that black people really were human.

Mary expressed her new conviction in the title of her book *The Australian Aboriginal as a Human Being* (1930). In the Australian outback, it was still a provocative and controversial thesis.

While Mary Bennett was working on her book, a group of police officers and settlers went into the Forrest River reserve in Kimberley and killed all the Aborigines they could find. When Pastor Gribble discovered and reported the mass murder, threats were made on his life. An investigation revealed that at least eleven Aborigines had been shot, probably while in chains. The perpetrators could not be convicted because no whites were prepared to testify against them, although they boasted openly of what they had done. The police officers returned to their duties with full authority. Pastor Gribble, on the other hand, was transferred elsewhere.[93]

The following year, 1928, the great drought in central Australia led to disputes over water. The Aborigines tried to stop the whites letting their cattle drink and pollute the water they needed for their own survival. A white dingo hunter named Brooks was murdered, giving the police the excuse to massacre the Aborigines indiscriminately. They were shot by the same policemen appointed to be their protectors. In this case, too, police action was found to have been justified, although the Aborigines who had been killed were innocent of Brooks' murder.[94]

In the end, the only guilty party was deemed to be one Sister Lock, who had been working among the native women and children of the area for twenty-five years. An investigation found her to be 'a woman missionary living amongst native blacks, thus lowering their respect for the whites', and her conduct was said to be the primary cause of the incident.[95]

Mary Bennett appealed to the growing number of enlightened, humane Australians shocked by the administration of such 'justice'. She was supported by both British and Australian women's organizations when, at the age of fifty, newly widowed, she returned to Australia to devote the rest of her life to the struggle for Aboriginal rights, especially those of the women.[96]

Personally I have never taken much interest in so-called 'blood ties'. My paternal grandmother Anna and my uncle Gustav have been important people in my life, as have my parents, daughter, son and grandson. But I've never understood why my siblings and my parents' brothers and sisters and their children and grandchildren should necessarily be any closer to me than my friends and their children and grandchildren.

I'm not tone-deaf. But I may be a little kin-deaf.

I ponder this as I drive south along the coastal road to Geraldton. Here, in 1945 in a sand dune behind the hospital, a girl named Millicent was born.[97]

From the word go, Little Milli was handicapped in kinship terms. Both her parents were 'half-castes', i.e. they had white fathers, who normally do not acknowledge any responsibility towards black children or grandchildren. So Milli lacked a grandfather on both sides. Their part of the family tree was totally unknown to her.

The black hole expanded and swallowed up everything. In 1949, since Milli was relatively fair-skinned, she was taken from her mother and father, her six brothers and sisters and the rest of her relations. At the age of four she was put into Sister Kate's Children's Home in Perth, and not permitted to see her family again or hear any news of them.

That same year saw the publication in Paris of Claude Lévi-Strauss's epoch-making dissertation *Les structures élémentaires de la parenté* (*Elementary Structures of Kinship*, 1949). He builds on Radcliffe-Brown's genealogical tables and is fascinated by the intricate patterns that emerge when the concept of 'paternity' also embraces uncles' wives' brothers and brothers-in-law's uncles. He sees the Aborigines' kinship culture not as a kind of social insurance but as an art form.

Perhaps different civilizations have chosen to develop different aspects of human life, he writes. Greek antiquity reached its zenith in drama and sculpture, our own civilization in technology and the control of nature. Australia's Aborigines chose instead to develop kinship relations and in them reached 'le point culminant de leur civilisation'.[98]

But in Geraldton they didn't read Lévi-Strauss. No one realized it was the culmination of a whole civilization they were violating when they tore apart the kinship network around Milli. They just took her.

'Child Welfare said we would have a better life and future brought up as whitefellas away from our parents in a good religious environment. All they contributed to our upbringing was an unrepairable scar of loneliness, mistrust, hatred and bitterness.'

The sibling group was systematically split up and sent to different institutions. Milli's brother Colin was placed in another section of Sister Kate's Home, so the children would meet only rarely. Sunday was visiting day. But their families never came.

'We spent each Sunday crying and comforting one another as we waited for our family. Each time was the same – no one came. That night we would cry ourselves to sleep and wonder why.'

The intention was clear: to make the children feel rejected and abandoned, thus crushing the very core of their Aboriginality. 'They told me that my family didn't care or want me and I had to forget them. They said it was very degrading to belong to an Aboriginal family and that I should be ashamed of myself.'[99]

Ashamed of what was her birth and her innermost sense of belonging. Ashamed of everything she was.

To become what?

66

At sixteen, Millicent was sent to a station as a maid. It soon transpired that her employer also expected sexual services. 'The man of the house used to come into my room at night and force me to have sex. I tried to fight him off but he was too strong.'

She fled to Sister Kate and told the whole story. After several clips round the ear, she had her mouth washed out with soap and was ordered back to the station. She prayed and begged to be excused, but to no avail. 'This time I was raped, bashed and slashed with a razor blade on both of my arms and legs because I would not stop struggling and screaming. The farmer and one of his workers raped me several times.'

She was sent back to 'the Home' and once more told them everything. She was beaten, had her mouth washed with soap again and was kept isolated from the other girls. 'They constantly told me that I was bad and a disgrace and that if anyone knew, it would bring shame on Sister Kate's Home.'

When it became apparent that she was pregnant, she received further beatings. 'My baby was taken away from me just as I was from my mother.'

This happened in 1962. It happened in one of the Anglo-Saxon democracies, under a freely elected government carefully scrutinized by a free press. It was one among tens of thousands of similar fates suffered by children of the 'stolen generations'.

It is not clear from Millicent's testimony whether she finally got to see her parents and siblings again. Was she ever able to reconnect with the extended vascular system of kinship relations that is the circulating blood of her people's social life? The only thing we know is that in 1996 Milli received an unexpected enquiry from the South Australian authorities concerning a woman, born in 1962, who was searching for her mother. It turned out to be Milli's daughter Tony. The two have now been reunited after thirty-four years without family, without kin, without belonging anywhere.

67

What is it that makes us into human beings? That was the great question which Darwin posed and Freud, Durkheim and the rest of the class of 1913 tried to answer with reference to the Australian Aborigines.

Claude Lévi-Strauss took up the challenge issued by his eminent predecessors. His answer was that reciprocity (*réciprocité*) was the key to humanity and civilization. If I give you a gift, you owe me a gift in return. The mutual exchange of gifts is the creative act that makes an animal into a human. Reciprocity is the common principle behind war and peace, trade and marriage – in brief, the premise on which all social life is based. The principle manifested itself first and most distinctly in the kinship system of the Aborigines.

This was not an entirely new idea.[100] But no one argued the case of reciprocity with more tenacity and rhetorical imagination than Lévi-Strauss. Nor did anyone else have his pretensions.

Lévi-Strauss does not study relationships between people and groups of people, but models resembling economists' ideal models of market functions.[101] Like many economists, Lévi-Strauss and his adherents believe the study of models offers knowledge of a deeper, truer reality than experience, which is all too often contaminated by specific circumstances. 'To reach reality one has first to reject experience.'[102]

To make anthropology properly scientific, Rivers wanted in 1910 to limit it to what can be studied using the self-checking 'genealogical method'. In 1949, Lévi-Strauss goes one step further and limits his branch of science to studying models of hypothetical genealogies. With the Aborigines' kinship terms as his building blocks, he creates a world of his own, free from all contradictions and reference to other worlds. In the preface to the second edition of *Les structures élémentaires* (*Elementary Structures*, 1967), he writes: 'Is there any need to emphasize that this book is concerned exclusively with models and not with empirical realities?'[103]

68

Reciprocity as the defining characteristic of humanity sounds fine. But what did it mean in practice?

Lévi-Strauss's model is constructed, like all others, on certain assumptions. These assumptions are often forgotten, or remain unstated for other reasons, when the model is presented.

1. The reciprocity that creates societies is always a relationship between men. Only relationships between men are social. The male–female relationship is biological, and relationships between women are not worth mentioning.
2. The reciprocity that creates societies presupposes men's power over women, particularly a father's and a brother's power to control and give away a daughter or sister.

When male animals learned to exchange goods and other useful articles with each other, they became human beings and created societies. The most highly valued exchange article, that which renders life possible and enjoyable for man, is woman. Exchange of sisters is therefore the origin of society.

The basis for symbolic thought, and human culture in general, is the uniquely human phenomenon of a man being able to enter into a relationship with another man by exchanging women with him.

Two boys meet, and get on well together. Each has a sister at his disposal. They agree to give each other their sisters as wives, once the girls reach sexual maturity. The two brothers-in-law thereby create between them an alliance that begins to work immediately, often many years before the agreed marriages take place. This alliance is, according to Lévi-Strauss, the concrete expression of reciprocity and the very core of society.

'It is no exaggeration to say that this is the archetype of all other manifestations of reciprocity, and is the basic, immutable rule assuring the existence of the group as a group.'

'The prohibition of incest is less a rule forbidding marriage to mother, sister or daughter, than a rule obliging a man to give away his daughter, sister or mother to others. It is the rule of gift-giving *par excellence*.'[104]

A woman can be seen, according to Lévi-Strauss, from two incompatible points of view. On the one hand she is an object for my, the man's, needs and arouses sexual desire in me. On the other hand, I note that she arouses the same desire in other men, therefore offering me the possibility of entering into alliance with them. The prohibition of incest means that I am obliged to choose the alliance over immediate sexual gratification. And I get the beginnings of a society into the bargain.

The idea that the woman herself might have some inclination in one direction or another is totally ignored. The rules of marriage are intended to satisfy 'a deeply rooted polygamous tendency found in all men'.[105]

By not using his own sisters and daughters sexually but instead giving them away in marriage, the man enters into an alliance with other men, creates society and holds it together.

How do we know this? Lévi-Strauss does not claim that any brother consciously finds himself in the situation of choosing between two different ways of using his sister. The assertion deals only with the – for the brother – unknown, unconscious significance of marrying off his sister. But Lévi-Strauss has no anthropological equivalent to psychoanalysis that could make the Aborigines' unconscious principles knowable to him.

His own unconscious principles are almost comically sexist.[106] Women are viewed only as resources owned by men. Their needs are treated as non-existent or negligible. Women's needs are satisfied within the biological family; it's men's needs that demand the formation of societies. If we want societies, we have to accept the rule of fathers and brothers, ultimately even honour killing. That's the logical conclusion of Lévi-Strauss's modelling.

When forcible treatment on the islands off Carnarvon ended in 1918, the buildings were pulled down and taken to Moore River north of Perth. They formed the basis for the Moore River Native Settlement, a school for children who had been taken from their black mothers. Under the leadership of the Aborigines' Chief Protector, Octavius Neville, nicknamed 'the Devil' by the Aborigines, Moore River became Western Australia's equivalent of the dreaded Kahlin Compound in Darwin.[107]

Neville was a competent man of many parts. He sang in choirs, played golf and loved gardening. His policy was to let the 'full-bloods' die out. There was no point trying to civilize them. The 'half-bloods', on the other hand, needed saving. He considered his authority to extend to anyone with the least drop of Aboriginal blood in their veins: they were to be isolated and controlled. In 1944, he summed up his philosophy as follows: 'The native must be helped in spite of himself! . . . the end in view will justify the means employed.'[108]

White people wished to avoid being disturbed by black people living nearby, while still having access to a supply of cheap black labour. Neville's solution was the remote agricultural colony at Moore River, where up to a quarter of Western Australia's Aborigines congregated, in an attempt to maintain contact with abducted children and grandchildren. The children were kept hard at work in preparation for their future jobs as servants and agricultural workers for the whites, and were also expected to contribute to their upkeep, to minimize the cost to the taxpayer.

The native colony functioned like the poorhouses of old.

Sparing use of public money was its guiding principle from the start. In 1921, its budget was reduced still further. The teachers' wages were cut. All 'unnecessary' equipment such as toys and modelling clay was removed and the curriculum was reduced to nothing but physical labour. The need to be economical also had an impact on the nutritional value of the food. A worryingly large number of Aborigines in Moore River began to suffer from tuberculosis. Doctors were only called out in rare, special cases, dentists never. Anyone with toothache had their teeth pulled by the camp director.[109]

Children were in a particularly vulnerable position. They often had no idea where they had come from or where their parents and relations were. The administrative routine was to allocate the children new names when they arrived at Moore, which made it difficult for parents to make contact with them. The staff told the children that their parents had lost interest in them, and told the parents their children didn't want to see them.

The staff weren't allowed to discuss conditions in the camp with outsiders. Breaking the rule meant instant dismissal. The staff read and censored all outgoing and incoming post. The camp director decided himself whether any complaints about his regime would be dealt with by him or forwarded to the Native Affairs department. In either case, it was rare for any action to be taken.

70

The only person who dared to take issue with the great maker of policy on native affairs, Octavius Neville, was Mary

Bennett. In a speech to the Commonwealth Conference of 1933 she condemned everything Moore River stood for, demanding that:

- Children of white fathers should not be taken from their black mothers to be brought up in institutions
- Young women should not be sent out as unpaid maids and risk being sexually assaulted by white employers
- Those appointed as the girls' guardians should be women, not policemen, who abused their power and turned a blind eye to other men doing the same
- The root of the native problem was that white and black male domination combined to produce dual oppression of women.

The speech prompted an official inquiry. For the first time ever, Aborigines from all over Western Australia came forward to give evidence. But since the testimonies came from 'natives', they had no official weight as evidence according to Australian law, so were never published. The truth remained in the archives.

The Aboriginal witnesses particularly criticized conditions at Moore. Visiting unannounced, the head of the inquiry found the buildings overcrowded and crawling with vermin. The children received no training for their future jobs. Their diet lacked fruit, vegetables, eggs and milk, with detrimental effects on their health. He concludes that the practice of lock-ing small children up in detention was barbaric.

But in spite of all this, the final report was brief and glossed over many aspects. The head of the inquiry found no proof of maltreatment of the Aborigines. Neville triumphed, and the Native Administration Act of 1937 legalized a number of his

To Pinjarra

earlier practices. The Chief Protector was given the explicit right to designate absolutely anyone, usually a white police-man, to carry out medical examinations of both sexes. Those who refused to be examined by the designated person could be punished by up to two years in prison. This enshrined in law the right of the police to harass and humiliate.

In order not to find themselves 'under the Act', children with parents of different races had to sever all contact with indigenous parents and kin. They could only marry with the Protector's permission. Neville had thus ensured he had the legal instruments to 'breed out' the Aborigines of Western Australia, which he saw as 'the final solution' to 'the race prob-lem'.[110]

Mary Bennett untiringly continued her campaign. She was there in 1938 when the Aborigines marked the 150th anniver-sary of the white invasion with a Day of Mourning, when she took the opportunity to voice further sharp criticism of Neville.

Neville retired in 1940, but the institution at Moore River remained open until 1951, and was later run by the Methodist Church under the name of Mogumber Mission. Today it is called Mogumber Farm, and the Aborigines run it them-selves. It became widely known through Doris Pilkington's documentary novel *Follow the Rabbit-Proof Fence* (1996) and the film *Rabbit-Proof Fence* (2002). Today there are plans to turn the former reform camp into a memorial to a dark era in Aboriginal history.

Moore River Native Settlement north of Perth had its equivalent to the south of the city in Carrolup Native Settlement. The official justification for the two institutions was the education they offered mixed-race children.

The school at Moore had just one teacher to teach more than a hundred children of different ages. Play was considered inappropriate and the teacher was severely criticized by the camp director for taking the children on nature walks after school. The children were to be set to work instead, then locked in their dormitories at 7.30. The children slept and worked in the same clothes all year round. None of them had shoes. Their food consisted of porridge for breakfast, soup for lunch and tea with bread and jam for supper.[111]

At Carrolup there was a schoolhouse of sorts, a concrete bunker with minimal equipment. The teacher's house was a tin hut with no kitchen or bathroom, and a paraffin lamp as the sole source of light. Nobody who could possibly get employment anywhere else took a job like that. At times when there was no teacher, the children hung about aimlessly all day and were locked into their dormitories at five o'clock, summer or winter.

In 1945, a couple named White heard about this 'dumping ground for human refuse',[112] and applied for the teaching post. Noel White had an unusual way of winning the children's confidence. He played the flute for them, and began with singing, drama, games and drawing. Looking in the school archive at the children's exercise books from before White's arrival, one finds nothing to indicate any hint of talent. For that reason, many outsiders believed that White was doing their drawings himself. But White couldn't draw, only inspire. He accustomed the children to drawing pictures of everything they learned about. The results were both comical and remarkably vivid.

At the children's request, White continued their schooling even after dark. No more being locked in their dormitories at five. By the light of the paraffin lamp, White told them about black people who had been guides for Eyre and other white 'discoverers', and about other contributions the Aborigines had made to the history of Australia. He encouraged them to listen to their old folk and learn as much as they could about their people's myths and legends. He taught the children to be proud of their black ancestry.[113]

The result of this teaching was a stream of increasingly interesting drawings, which created a stir in Perth and were a great success in London, where they were exhibited in June 1950.

What does one do with children who win international acclaim though they are nothing but refuse? They can never become real artists, after all. Maybe they should be taught to draw advertisements? Or take other jobs and pursue their artistic interests in their free time? And who actually owned the artwork that had already been produced and sold? The children? Or their parents, or maybe the Education Department or the Native Affairs Department?

The girls were sent to a Catholic missionary school, where they were taught sewing instead of art. A few particularly gifted boys were given jobs as office boys in the Education Department in Perth. They soon got bored and longed to get home to White and their classmates in Carrolup. But there, the media interest in the young artists had provoked a power struggle between White and the new school management, which was doing all it could to lure the boys away from the teacher's influence. Art was pushed aside to make way for sport and scouting. It took the new director a year to have Noel White sacked, the school closed and the children dispersed.[114]

72

The girls from Carrolup became maids or prostitutes; the boys often got work at local vineyards. Part of their wages was paid in wine; before long they would have committed some crime while under the influence and begun their careers as jail-birds.[115]

Australia's first Aboriginal novel, Colin Johnson's *Wild Cat Falling* (1965), tells the story of a talented, proud and touchy young man, just released from prison in Fremantle.

His whole childhood and adolescence has been a struggle for acceptance as a white by the whites, a struggle to be white although he wasn't. So he was forbidden from playing with black children. He had to eat up his nice food like a good little white child. White was what you had to be. If you had the slightest hint of black in you, the Welfare would be down on you. 'You know what that'll mean.'

He knew, all right. The Welfare wanted to take him away from his mother. The Welfare was always on the lookout for children who weren't white enough. The Welfare wanted to take them from their homes to put them in 'homes'. And sure enough, at the age of nine he's caught, ends up in a 'boys' home' and then at Carrolup. And here he stands now, just out of prison.

He's scared. At least prison was a sort of refuge. He won some respect there, he was somebody. But out here?

The first person he meets is a white girl who advises him to start again. Which means: try to be white again. He plays it cool.

– I am too old now.
– How old?
– Nineteen.
– Practically Methuselah.
– Too old to laugh or cry any more. So old my bones ache . . .
– That's up to you.

I feel the old bitter taste of resentment in my mouth. Nothing is ever up to them. Only up to us, the outcast relics in the outskirt camps. The lazy, ungrateful rubbish people, who refuse to co-operate or integrate or even play it up for the tourist trade. Flyblown descendants of the dispossessed erupting their hopelessness in petty crime . . .[116]

He's soon back with the old gang, planning a new theft to prove prison hasn't 'reformed' him. They steal a car and make themselves scarce, go back to his old home town. But the break-in is discovered, they have nothing to show for their pains, and a shot is fired in the turmoil.

He flees into the woods and comes across an old black rabbit catcher he remembers from his childhood. He is told that his mother now lives in the Aboriginal camp.

She got nobody, only them, son.

Mum, with her phoney pride, dependent on the kindness of the people she reared me to despise. They brawl and bash each other up, gamble the shirts off their backs and make fools of anyone who tries to help them, but they have a warmth and loyalty to each other and a sort of philosophy of life that whites will never know or understand.[117]

He sleeps in the old man's hut and, seeing his chance, steals some money from a bowl. As he's leaving, he is given a gift by the old man: the very money he has just stolen.

'I feel the blood flushing up my neck and over my face and I hang my head. No one has ever made me feel that way before. No one.'

For the author, as for the novel's narrator, *Wild Cat Falling* means he stops trying to be white and accepts his Aboriginal identity. Colin Johnson was the name the author used for his first novel, but it was as Mudrooroo that he became the leading novelist of Aboriginal literature.

73

How did it begin? Where did it begin?

The train rattles south through fertile, green agricultural land. There's a soft drizzle and all the furrows, hollows and depressions are full of water.

This is how green and inviting the country appeared to Captain James Stirling when he first stepped ashore in Western Australia in 1827. He thought he'd found paradise. He threw in his lot with young landowner Thomas Peel and set up a company that promised every immigrant twenty acres of land for £3. He was unaware of, or paid no heed to, the fact that the land was already owned and looked after by a people that knew all its secrets. For him, the whole lot was *terra nullius*.

The first settlers arrived in 1829 – with wholly unrealistic expectations of the life that awaited them. They got no further than the beach, freezing through the storms of winter, plagued by sandflies and mosquitoes in summer. Their dining-room furniture rotted in the rain as the allocation of land proceeded at an unbearable snail's pace. After a few years in tents by the beach, most had tired of it all and moved on to Sydney. One of the few who remained was Thomas Peel himself. He sat alone in a stone hut on his estate of 640 square kilometres.

I'm the only one who gets off at Pinjarra. Opposite the station lies the Premier Hotel. A bridge leads over the long valley of the Murray River. Then comes the little town, threaded along its main street like wild strawberries on a stalk of straw – post office and bank, police station and courthouse, café and pizzeria, tyres and petrol, Food Land and Farm Mart, newspaper shop and estate agent. Oh, and the churches, of course: the Anglican St John's, the Roman Catholic St Augustine's, plus Pinjarra Unity Church, the Alliance Church of Pinjarra and the Open Faces Christian Ministry.

The tourist office has its premises in Edenvale, a grand house in the classical style. Its brochure recommends a 'History Walk' through the town, but doesn't say a word about the only thing for which the place is famous. Only those who make a point of asking get the special little brochure produced in conjunction with the Murray District Aboriginal Association.

I look through the brochure over my lunch of cheese sandwiches and a pot of tea, then walk across the narrow, swaying suspension bridge over the river and follow the route along the bank through the park. According to one version of history, this was the site of the 'Battle of Pinjarra'. The other version calls it the 'Pinjarra Massacre'. Fifteen black warriors fell, says one story. According to the other, about a hundred black people, mostly women and children, were buried in three mass graves and thirteen individual graves.

In 1834, the first settlers had just begun taking possession of the rich areas of land in the Murray River valley. The Nyungar people resisted, under their local leader, Calyute. Peel had invested his fortune in this huge area of land which risked becoming worthless if the natives succeeded in scaring away the settlers. He called for military assistance from Governor Stirling.[118]

When Stirling seized the '*terra nullius*' on behalf of the British crown, he had declared the few (so he believed) Aborigines to be British subjects, with all the rights this implied. Now, five years later, ownership of the territory was disputed and violence seemed necessary, even commendable.

On 27 October 1834, Stirling left Thomas Peel's estate with eleven soldiers and five mounted policemen, as well as Peel himself and a pack of dogs. The ford at Pinjarra was known as a crossroads and meeting place for the natives. Stirling spent the night at a suitable distance from the ford, and attacked at dawn. Some eighty black people were taken completely by surprise. When they tried to run away, they came under fire from the main force, located higher up on the opposite bank. Those trying to escape downriver were shot by men stationed at the next ford.

The massacre was all over in an hour, but was followed by a protracted hunt in the surrounding brush. On the whites' side, one man had been injured, and one other thrown from the saddle by native spears. According to the Aborigines, half the

Nyungar people was killed, and its existence as a social entity was destroyed.

Once the two top men of the colonization project had given the lead, there was nothing to stop the rest of the settlers from following their example. The Pinjarra massacre unleashed a wave of terror that virtually annihilated black people the length of the Murray River valley.

The Smell of White Man

74

Early morning. I glide slowly and quietly out of Perth's urban landscape, into the farming belt – pale green autumn wheat and fields of grey stubble edged with white-trunked eucalyptus. Each tree is its own copse. Some are multi-storeyed, with different levels of foliage stacked one on top of the other, often with a cheeky little penthouse at the very top.

Road, railway and pipeline run alongside each other. The

water isn't running down from the mountains to the city with its million-plus inhabitants, but being pumped from a reservoir in Perth up to the mines in the goldfields on the desert rim.

I spend the night at Hotel Australian in Kalgoorlie, in a town centre where the renovated *fin de siècle* buildings still maintain the extravagant mood of the gold rush.

I go for a beer at the Exchange Hotel & Pub, opposite the Australian. It turns out to be the favoured haunt of the miners from New Zealand. For men with dreams of being cowboys, there are bar stools in the shape of saddles. Electronic horses offer virtual rodeo. There's not a woman in sight apart from the waitresses, who wear body stockings and are known as 'skimpies'.

Just round the corner is Paddy's Pub, where all the Irish go. An electronic disc jockey coordinates the blaring music with the gigantic video screen and a dozen smaller TV screens showing various sport channels, mostly boxing and racing. Then there's a billiard table and one of those old-fashioned but clearly hugely popular table football games where you flick the handles with your own bare hands to get the players to 'kick' the ball, without any interference from computer power or even electricity.

I ended up at Bodington's. The men's toilets there aren't marked 'Gentlemen' or even 'Gents', but 'Miners'.

75

The coldest night of the year in Kalgoorlie. The temperature fell below freezing. I slept with my outdoor clothes on. But the clear weather that made the night cold also makes the day warm.

In the course of today's drive I saw six black emus picking their way with great *gravitas* among pewter-grey tussocks of grass and silvery bluebushes which look as though they have a coating of hoar-frost. Also five wild camels, one of them creamy white, grazing on the white grass. But no kangaroos, or at least no live ones – I've seen more than enough dead ones, there must have been about thirty bodies, victims of a permanently ongoing traffic massacre.

Depressions with clumps of red grass in red sand. Rounded green bushes. Little balls of green thrown aloft by spindly tree-trunks. The wooded landscape gradually thins, the ground is bared, the plains open up – but it's not a proper desert, not yet.

Bacon and eggs at the Grand Hotel in Leonora. The smell of the food is so greasy you could fry the eggs in it. As I'm eating, the wind gets up from the west and heavy rainclouds fill the sky. I drive on with the wind at my back, and soon it's no longer cold but warm and humid.

At Laverton I check into the only hotel, the Desert Inn Hotel Motel. The narrow main entrance in the windowless wall makes me happy. Hotel entrances don't usually look like that. Hotels usually announce their names in huge letters over doors wide enough to admit the fattest of wallets. Not here. Here there's just a narrow door, and above it simply the word 'Entrance'.

The door leads straight into the bar, which although it's only three in the afternoon is full of rowdy, quarrelsome, drunken men with hats grafted to their heads. A fat girl opens the top half of the door to the 'office', which consists only of a board with keyhooks. I'm given the key to room 10, which is furnished with a hard bed, a hard chair, a bedside table and a glass for a toothbrush. And a number of tree branches for the wind to scrape endlessly to and fro over the tin roof.

Whites are drinking with whites in the bar, blacks with blacks. They pretend not to notice each other. The black people are watching dog and horse racing on television, faithfully staking their money in a betting machine before the start of every new race. By about six, Thursday evening in Laverton has begun. Only the hotel, the liquor store and the police station are still open.

A glance at the map shows me to be at about the same longitude as Fitzroy Crossing and the same latitude as Geraldton on the west coast. Between me and Coober Pedy to the east lies the Great Victoria Desert, Australia's largest. It has no water at all running on its surface, but beneath the sand dunes the bedrock is criss-crossed by riverbeds and drainage canals. The heart of the desert is so inaccessible that it has never been grazed by cattle, nor does it have any non-native flora.[119]

Laverton is at the end of a little appendix in the road network: I've reached 'the end of the road'. Just seeing a place like that on a map gives me an adrenalin rush. And to actually be here, to see map and reality coincide for a moment – what does it matter that the room is shabby, the lights dim, the food inedible? It matters not at all. I'm happy.

76

Cold morning. Ground frost on the bathroom floor. All the moisture from here to Alice Springs seems to have been collected together and released on to the dripping car. But the sun is close. Why does it always seem so much closer here than in Sweden? The sun in Australia never seems more than a couple of blocks away.

The roads into Leonora are all adorned with big notices exhorting truck drivers to clean their wheels before they drive into the town. Like little boys, they're told to wipe the mud off their boots before they come rushing in. When you see the deposits the truck wheels leave on the tarmac, you understand why. Everything is obliterated by the red dust: the broken line down the middle, the unbroken lines at the sides – it all disappears in the same red dust-dream and blends into the verges and surrounding land, making a homogeneous red universe without boundaries or direction. In the midst of it all there's a pub calling itself 'The Pub With No Beer'.

Slowly south through lovely forests around Lakes Lefroi and Cowan. Could they be described as shallow? Somehow, a certain depth is required for something to be shallow. Here, the lake is so utterly without depth that the moisture seems to have been licked over the ground as over the back of a postage stamp. These are lakes as thin as a covering of ice formed over-night. But to the eye they still make a glittering surface that from a distance looks like an ocean.

Norseman is a crossroads with well-kept roadhouses and a mine that has created a vast, grey-black slagheap above the town. It looks as if it could start to slip at any moment, come crashing down and wipe out the town.

We're used to equestrian statues with riders. In Norseman the statue features not the rider but the horse; that is, the horse which according to legend found gold here in 1893.

In my dream that night the polar bears gave a party for their human friends. They weren't aggressive at all, but of course you had to be careful. It's well known that white bears are more dangerous than brown ones. I spent most of my time up on the table, or on a shelf that ran round the wall. A polar bear in a uniform cap was acting as a policeman, but not unaided – behind him walked another police officer, a white person, to make sure the bear beheaded himself.

77

After Norseman, the road turns east. Between Belladonia and Caiguna comes the longest straight stretch in Australia, and presumably the world: 180 kilometres without a millimetre's deviation sideways or up and down.

The coastal desert is called the Nullarbor, 'No Trees'. All you see are occasional dried-up trees along the wayside, like those marker buoys with brooms sticking up. The last forest disappeared during a period of drought fifteen thousand years ago.

The history of the Nullarbor goes back to the time when Australia was part of Antarctica.[120] When the two continents went their separate ways hundreds of millions of years ago, the landscape was broken in two. Rivers that once ran from Antarctica into Australia continued in their previous course. Australia became unique in that the flow of water in its whole interior and on large parts of its south coast is not towards the sea but inwards to the basin floor. What were once rivers are now chains of thin salt lakes. The water from the irregular rains vanishes down into the limestone in this karst desert with its winding, undrained cirques.

When the world oceans rose and the sea level reached its

highest point, 116 million years ago, the Nullarbor and the whole interior of Australia were flooded. Fifty million years ago, the sea invaded again, creating layers of sediment. Thirty-six million years ago the sea receded, only to return twenty million years ago. Now the whole area was covered in limestone.

The Nullarbor is the world's largest limestone plateau, a quarter of a million square kilometres in size. Beneath the plateau there are caves, large and small, some eroded by the sea, others by streams of water from torrential rain in the interior of Australia. All caves breathe to some extent, and in the Nullarbor the breathing of the caves is particularly lively. They breathe in when the air pressure rises, and out when it falls. Air speeds of up to seventy-two kilometres an hour have been recorded.

The openings through which this breathing occurs are called 'blowholes'. Their sighs and groans have been the source of legends that the caves are inhabited, stories of subterranean cities and secret passageways to undiscovered gold deposits, of ancient peoples living on underground, defying time.

The desert is at its most desolate between the Nullarbor Roadhouse and Yalata. In the middle of the day, a red dust-storm comes sweeping along the coast. Wild gusts of wind tug at the car, the red vortex lifts debris from the ground and tosses it up in the air in whirling spirals. Trees and houses are shrouded in red mist. It's scarily beautiful; my heart contracts sharply in my chest, but nothing happens, and seconds later the vortex has moved on.

At Nundroo Roadhouse, where I stay the night, you're only permitted entry to the bar if you meet strict criteria for neat, tidy, clean dress, good personal hygiene, appropriate footwear, sobriety and unripped clothing. The management moreover reserves the right in each individual case to deny admission to those deemed to be behaving inappropriately.

I am woken several times during the night by violent cloud-bursts beating on the tin roof. Will the rain make the road impassable? Have I, in this area of extremely sparse rainfall, managed to coincide with the only day of the year when water floods the road out into the desert?

78

Heavy black clouds hang like udders from the sky; the ground is covered in pools of water and there's a light drizzle. I drive the fifty kilometres to Yalata in the dramatic lighting of the sunrise.

Then I turn north through Yalata Community, an Aboriginal settlement, where the tarmac gives way to a wash-board-like surface. The buzz is like driving across an endless cattle grid; the hard suspension makes the car body vibrate like a pneumatic drill.

After a long, bumpy stretch, the sand comes as a delightful, treacherous relief. The car is suddenly floating agreeably, like cream on top of milk. You're suspended. But that's also when you run the greatest risk of getting stuck, as your tyres dig into the sand. The potholes are easier to negotiate. You drive round them, of course, if you can. Otherwise you take your foot off the accelerator and let yourself swing down into the hole and up again.

I don't meet a soul on this stretch. I pass a score or more of wrecked cars at intervals along the road, showing it's not without its dangers. I carry on north through the ever more naked landscape I love. And suddenly I'm there. It's the railway. There's the first little signpost. It points west, to Watson, the next station. Straight on, heading north, the road goes up to Maralinga, a prohibited zone. A few hundred metres east stands the station sign: OOLDEA. The station house and the platforms have gone, all that remains is a little shunting yard with rusty rails and a small pile of concrete sleepers.

And there inside a ring of white stones is a white-painted lump of concrete bearing the words: '1859–1951 Mrs Daisy Bates CBE. Devoted her life here and elsewhere to the welfare of the Australian aborigines.'

No flowers, just thistles. The sun is shining and the wind is bitterly cold.

79

The Nullarbor is only the coastal strip of the vast Great Victoria Desert.[121] There are no springs. All life is dependent on a hundred or so watering places: depressions and hollows where the rainwater collects in natural dishes of hard clay. Some of these dishes are small and shallow, and quickly dry out. The biggest and most reliable was Ooldea. For that reason, Ooldea became one of the most important meeting points in the desert, a place on which all paths converged, where you could find refuge from the drought, where ceremonies with several hundred participants could be held without the water running out.

The supply of water also led to Ooldea becoming a junction on the transcontinental railway that was built in 1912–17. That was where the railway construction project advancing from the east met the one coming from the west. That was where the locomotives filled their water tanks, whether they were east-bound or west-bound. The railway used forty-five metric tons of water a day. As the wells ran dry, new and deeper ones were dug, until one day in 1922 the company engineers bored down into the bowl-like cavity that retained the water, and cracked it. It had taken modern technology ten years to destroy a natural resource many thousands of years old.

The water now had to be transported in tank wagons as rail freight, primarily for railway use, secondarily for the needs of white settlers along the railway. In third place, and only if supplies permitted, it was provided for the black people whose watering places had been destroyed. They congregated around the station in their hundreds to beg for water. Soon enough, they were begging for food and money too. Soon enough, the railway passengers realized that they could invite little black girls on board, get them drunk, abuse them and throw them off further down the line – where they had no choice but to prostitute themselves again for a free ride back to Ooldea. Within a few years, alcohol and syphilis broke down the Aborigines who had come from the desert healthy and well nourished.

Daisy Bates was convinced the indigenous peoples of Australia were bound for extinction.[122] Her time as Radcliffe-Brown's scientific handmaid on the Islands of the Dead had strengthened her in that conviction. Back in Perth, she set out to look for the surviving remnants of the once numerous Bibulmun people. In Hopetown there was no hope left: they had already died out. In Esperance things didn't look hopeful either: there was just one old pair of brothers left, known as Dib and Dab. Everyone said, '*Jangga meenya bomunggur*' – 'The smell of white man is killing us.'[123]

She applied for a position as the natives' Protector, but the post was considered too hazardous for a woman.[124] Instead, she immersed herself in the Aborigines' world unpaid and unprotected. Her tent could be observed at Eucla and Yalata as the First World War raged and media attention was directed elsewhere. During the visit of the Prince of Wales in 1920, his train stopped at Ooldea to take on water, and Daisy found herself briefly front-page news. Then she disappeared into obscurity again for over a decade.

But the easterly sirocco hadn't forgotten her. It carried on storing sand between her sheets and under her eyelids. 'A geologist could have made a study of the landscapes I have seen using the dust they have left in my eyes.'[125]

When she returned to the white world at the age of seventy-six, she prepared herself carefully for the transition. 'It had to be done in stages, like a diver in one of those metal capsules being slowly raised from the depths of the ocean, lying still while he gets used to the unaccustomed weight of the air around him.'[126]

Daisy Bates had never been to the cinema; she refused to speak on the telephone and pretended to be deaf when the radio was on. But after all those years in the desert, she loved interviews and photographers. She wanted to be the centre of attention. Well into her eighties, she would flirt wildly with the men around her.[127]

She brought with her a ton of paperwork, which was deposited in the library of the *Advertiser*, the newspaper that sponsored her return. The journalist Ernestine Hill tried in vain to retrieve anything publishable from the chaos. The diaries generally petered out after the first few months of each year, ending in heat and urgency, burden of work and lack of events. All the material was already old. They had to start all over again and proceed orally. Bates told her story; Hill made

notes. 'All the material was hers; only the arranging, formula-
tion and the writing itself was mine,' said Hill half a century
later.

How did she bear it, year after year in the monotony of the
desert, through winter storms and summer heat? What did she
really do for the natives? What was the value of her research?
How could she reconcile her belief in the extinction of the
indigenous people with her belief in the benevolence of the
empire and the white woman's burden? What were the origins
of her less than healthy tendency to share with other people
and give away everything she had?

Her book *The Passing of the Aborigines* (1938) offers no
answer to these crucial questions. More than forty years after
her death, Daisy Bates remains an enigma.

80

The authorities viewed Daisy Bates's activities in Ooldea with
the utmost suspicion, and came up with a constant stream of
imaginative excuses for ordering her to leave. But when the
United Aborigines Mission opened a mission station on the
ritual site beside the former waterhole, they received full backing from the authorities. The missionaries were authorized to
hand out state rations of flour, sugar, tea and tobacco to the
natives. The natives were also attracted to the school, although
the girls were locked in their dormitories each evening and
could only see their parents for a few hours a week. The
parents had to adhere to a strict code of dress – no Aborigine
could approach the mission unless dressed like a white person.

The Smell of White Man

It was the missionaries' stated intention to break down the traditional culture which in their eyes was heathen superstition. Their first aim was to undermine the authority of the clan system. One method employed was to take lantern slides of holy objects and symbols which the old men had loaned out on condition the missionaries kept them confidential, and then show the slides to the schoolboys with comments such as 'Look how stupid this is! Just some old bits of wood! How can anyone think they're important! Don't listen to those silly old men, they don't know anything.'

The missionaries saw themselves as saviours when they 'protected' the boys from the horrors of circumcision and the whole barbaric cultural heritage surrounding it. They urged the boys to marry before their people considered them mature enough for such responsibility.

The missionaries saw themselves as saviours when they 'protected' the girls from being married off as third concubine to some old man their uncle had chosen for them. They urged the girls to break their tribal laws and marry one of the boys who had 'seen the light' and whom the missionaries had chosen for them.

Catherine and Ronald Berndt, who later became well-known anthropologists, carried out their first fieldwork in Ooldea in 1941. In their report *From Black to White* (1951), they criticize the mission for confusing Christianity with European middle-class mores. The missionaries didn't realize how coercive their practices were. The youths growing up in the dormitories were subjected throughout their most impressionable years to a barrage of propaganda against the culture of their own people. Their ultimate aspiration was supposed to be conversion to Christianity and marriage that contravened the laws of their people.

'Last Sunday there were great preparations, for we had the joy of marrying in our little church yet another Christian couple: Albert Amunga and Meda Odewa were joined in the Lord after yet another hard struggle against the customs and laws of the tribe. Everything went very well, photographs were taken and the young couple drank tea with all the missionaries. It was a pleasant evening.'[128]

But the next day there was trouble, and a few days later Odewa's parents took her down to the coast, out of reach of the missionaries, who could only hope she would one day be reunited with Amunga.

It simply wasn't possible to pick and choose between elements of the two cultures. Saying no to traditional marriage meant breaking with your family, kin and nation. Saying no to Christian marriage meant forgoing the social and economic advantages the mission and its wider society had to offer.

Behind both alternatives, catastrophe loomed. Both seemed to be on a collision course with the railway and everything it brought with it. Both whites and blacks were convinced the collision would lead to the destruction of the blacks. The mission saw cultural destruction in a positive light, as salvation from physical destruction. The two anthropologists hoped instead for cultural renewal. But in what form?

Len Beadell, who in the 1940s had transformed the Great Victoria Desert into an enormous missile-firing range, was given a new task at the start of the 1950s: to find a suitable location for the testing of British atomic weapons.

What was required for white culture to live out its suicidal tendencies was a site about ten kilometres in diameter, free from obstructing sand dunes and far enough away from the launch pads for the radiation from the test bombs not to interfere with the missile experiments.

The place initially chosen was Emu, where a ten-kiloton atomic bomb was detonated on 15 October 1953. The radioactive cloud rose to a height of 4,500 metres and then moved across the continent for forty-eight hours. At the press conference, someone said the bomb cloud looked like an Aborigine: 'A perfect portrait of a myall blackfellow written with atomic dust; the new and the old have come together today.'[129] The words were front-page headlines in all the papers.

It was the natives whose lives were put most at risk. It was their land that was contaminated. The problem then was to keep them away from their old paths and ritual sites and warn them of an invisible danger that could only be measured by Geiger counters.

The most urgent step was to close down the mission in Ooldea. The missionaries were evacuated in 1952, the Aborigines stayed. A Lutheran missionary from Koonibba was given orders to travel there and bring fifty dormitory children back with him. Only six came. Of the three hundred adults he had orders to transport to Yalata, only sixty-five came voluntarily.

The rest were evacuated by force, or vanished into the vast 'prohibited area' into which the former reservation was transformed.

After two large and numerous smaller atomic-weapon tests, Emu had become too dangerous. Len Beadell was sent out to look for a new location, and happened upon Ooldea, now abandoned. There, the clear-felled sand dunes had begun to shift and bury the buildings. Drifts of sand were blocking the outer doors and getting in through the windows.

A new town was laid out just west of Ooldea: Maralinga, with a thousand inhabitants, a hospital and an airport. At the test site a short distance away, seven British atomic bombs were set off in 1956–7. What the British called 'minor trials' continued until 1963, in spite of the Nuclear Test Ban Treaty. The minor trials were of three different kinds: 'Kittens' tested different methods of setting off an atom bomb; 'Rats' tested different materials used in atom bombs; and finally 'Vixens' studied the consequences of nuclear accidents, such as fires in nuclear-weapon stores or the crash-landing of a plane carrying an atomic weapon.

It was these six hundred or so 'minor trials' that had the most serious repercussions. Over twenty kilos of plutonium was spread over large areas in the form of fine dust. The particles are dangerous if eaten or inhaled. People who go naked and barefoot, live in the open air, drink from open waterholes and gather their food from the ground or just under it are, of course, particularly vulnerable.

We don't know how much dangerous material is left today in Maralinga and its environs. Seven tons of uranium, 830 tons of atomic waste and 1,120 tons of contaminated sand are buried in twenty-six protective pits in the area. Of the ninety-nine kilos of beryllium that was dispersed in Maralinga, less than two kilos has been retrieved and removed.[130]

Repeated decontamination projects were undertaken in the mid-1960s; in 1968 an agreement was signed freeing the British government from further liability for any results of the atomic tests.

Ten years later, the area was re-examined. The British decontamination was found to have consisted of ploughing the plutonium a few decimetres below the surface of the ground, where it had soon been laid bare by the fierce desert winds.

The Australian Nuclear Veterans' Association was set up in 1979. Hundreds of experts and others involved in the experiments told of their experiences. The British sent three Hercules planes to continue the decontamination process, but only managed to retrieve half a kilo of plutonium. At least nineteen kilos remained lying in the desert sands.

By the Maralinga Land Rights Act of 1983, the new Labor government gave the indigenous people back the land that had been requisitioned from them in the fifties. But how safe was it to move back there?

A Royal Commission was appointed in 1984. It heard 311 witnesses and drew 201 conclusions, leading to 7 recommendations. The commission made the British solely responsible for the decontamination of the ground and demanded that the area be made safe for permanent settlement by the native inhabitants.

While the commission was at work, fences and warning signs were erected. They were still there at the beginning of the twenty-first century. The half-life of the radioactivity in the plutonium is 280,000 years.

And the nuclear weapons that had been developed had a combined destructive power equivalent to a million Hiroshima bombs. On a single order, the entire world can be turned into *terra nullius*.

The Ground

Yuendumu
Utopia
Kintore
Kiwirkurra
Papunya
Alice Springs
Hermannsburg
Simpson Desert
Uluru
Ernabella
reat Victoria
Desert
Stuart Highway
Maralinga
Ooldea
Nullarbor Desert
Woomera
Yalata
Ceduna

83

I see black fern patterns in light sand. I see light ribs on a dark background – an opened chest cavity. I see salt lakes lathered like half-scrubbed wooden floors.

I'm aboard a taxi plane, taking the short-cut across the

Great Victoria Desert from Ceduna to Alice Springs. It saves me three days covering a route I've already driven. Above all, it gives me a new vantage point.

I look down over a dry inland lake, bluey-white with salt that could almost be ice. I see an archipelago of red islands in an Antarctic of salt.

The ground is striped and fingered, full of riverbeds without rivers. Criss-crossed by innumerable runnels that aren't running anywhere, traces of water events that used to happen once but aren't happening any more. A history wholly characterized by its landscape. A landscape wholly characterized by its history, or to be more precise, its water history. You feel you could read the ground as Sherlock Holmes reads the scene of a crime.

The bulldozers have left behind a few straight, red tracks in the ash-grey sand and white salt. Wind and water have left behind innumerable, meandering tracks, branching and rejoining each other, in nature's marshalling yard.

Little spots of yellow sand in the salt, like the yolk in a fried egg. Furrows, ploughed by water. Ditches, dug by wind. Salt warp in the woven fabric. The shapes recur at regular intervals, as if in a wallpaper design.

From up here, it can be hard to see where the desert ends and the sky begins, when the sand cover and the cloud cover are the same colour. The horizon seems to be lying sometimes right at your feet, so you almost stumble over it, sometimes way up at the zenith.

The trailing light of evening accentuates the sandy ridges; the edges grow sharper, the shadows deeper. But the clarity of focus only lasts a moment. Then the colours pale, and fade out. Everything is erased in a froth of deep pink dusk.

We've arrived.

Why weren't the Aborigines who had been evacuated to Yalata content to stay there? Why was it so desperately important for them to return to exactly the same lands where they had lived before, although those were the very areas that were now contaminated with radioactivity?

The white authorities could understand that farmers might be attached to the soil. But the Aborigines weren't farmers. They were nomads. Who ever heard of a deeply rooted nomad? No, unlimited mobility was part of the nomad concept.

So the Aborigines were constantly being moved, not only to allow for atom-bomb tests, but also because the whites' cattle needed a particular pool of water or because the whites' company had found new mineral deposits – or simply for their own good, so they could be looked after and learn the whites' table manners, the whites' good home cooking, the whites' working hours. The new policy after the Second World War was aimed at 'assimilating' the Aborigines, which didn't imply white people thought they had anything to learn from black people, but meant black people were to be trained to be steady wage earners and consumers on the fringes of white society.

Out in the desert, Aborigines were rounded up by police patrols that took them to mission stations like Ernabella or Hermannsburg, or to state internment camps like Papunya and Yuendumu. One nigger was as good as another; nobody was bothered that they belonged to different nations and spoke dozens of different languages. After all, no proper person could tell those languages apart.

It was equally incomprehensible that every Aborigine had

custody of particular places out in the desert and had to return to them to carry out their religious ceremonies – though the 'place' to white eyes looked just the same as all the other places in the desert. Employers and camp directors suspected that all the talk of 'holy places' was just an invention of incurable vagabonds and deserters from the settled lifestyle the internment camps were trying to teach.

85

White society was constructed on the presumption that Australia at the time of the British invasion had been 'no one's land'. Along the coasts, where the British first arrived, the continent was admittedly populated, but deeper inland they visualized vast, uninhabited tracts. Countless explorers traversed Australia in all directions, vainly seeking the no man's land that was needed to legitimize the invasion.

In the end, only the deserts at the heart of the continent were left. Clearly there was little appetite for admitting that even here, where the land was least accessible and hospitable, even here every stone, every bush and every waterhole had its specific owner and custodian, its sacred history and religious significance.

The main thrust of white research on the subject of the Aborigines therefore avoided sacred geography. Spencer and Gillen took an interest in how people related to animals, Radcliffe-Brown in how they related to one another. No one showed an interest in the relationship between the people and their land.

Spencer and Gillen let the subjects of their study move to the back yards of the telegraph station, so they were easily accessible. Radcliffe-Brown found the subjects of his study among the involuntary in-patients languishing on the Islands of the Dead, far from their homelands. No wonder they missed the significance of place. The vantage point they had selected made place invisible.

86

Theo Strehlow (1909–78) chose a different vantage point.[131] He was the only white child in Hermannsburg where his father, Carl Strehlow, was a missionary. Theo grew up in the borderland between two languages and cultures. His black playmates ran about naked and free, played wherever they wanted and were never beaten. He himself had a strict German Lutheran upbringing. Children were little animals who must be tamed by a lovingly brutal father figure. If he said anything wrong in German, he was punished. The language of his playmates and the maids, Arrernte, became his true maternal tongue.

After Strehlow's father died in 1922, mother and son moved to Adelaide, where Theo's unique linguistic skills aroused attention at his school and then at the university. In 1932, his professor sent him back to Hermannsburg to study the phonetics of the Arrernte language. After a period of scientific fieldwork, he got a job as a mounted policeman, spending a total of fifteen years in the wilds. He was the only white man who could speak to the tribesmen in their own language, the only one who had no need of an interpreter to understand their songs and stories.

He sought them out wherever they happened to be, *in situ*, amidst the geography that also contained their history. For a people without documents, history soon turns into fairy tale and dream. But the geography remains. You can't travel through history, but you can go to the place where the past happened. Soon you don't know any more when it happened, only where it happened and where it goes on happening.

'It cannot be stressed too strongly that Central Australian mythology did not concern itself with the sky but with the ground,' said Strehlow towards the end of his life, when he drew together his knowledge of what he called the 'totemic landscape'.[132]

Here, as so often, he is in dialogue with his father. Carl Strehlow had always looked for an equivalent to the heavenly God of Christianity in the natives' songs and tales. But his son emphasizes a human being's connection with the ground in his place of origin, and with the supernatural beings that created it and still live there. Mythology is an imprint of the landscape and can only be understood fully by someone who has experienced the places described in the myth.

This 'ground-based religion' was the motor of economic life. Without ceremonies, the ground would dry out, animal prey would disappear, roots and seeds would shrivel. A religious leader's function was similar to that of a minister of agriculture and food: to ensure growth, to prepare the ground for small-scale enterprises in family groups, to create the right business climate for gathering and hunting.

Theo Strehlow also investigated the network of tracks and pathways that crossed the Simpson and Victoria Deserts. The Aborigines' constant migrations in their forefathers' footsteps enabled them to exploit local resources that would soon have been exhausted by permanent settlements. The intersections on the network had great economic importance as trading places. But above all they were holy places where historical myths were kept alive.

The holy sites of the Christian religion, from Bethlehem to Golgotha, are for most Christians very distant. In central Australia, the holy places have an uncommonly personal intimacy. The eternal truths of religion are expressed in the surrounding landscape. One can go to these truths, set up camp among them, become pregnant by them, draw them on the ground, dance them and sing them, in the very spot where they once occurred – and thereby keep them alive and, along with many other people, contribute to keeping the whole universe alive.

87

Theo Strehlow saw himself as the Homer of the Arrernte people.[133] His ambition was to combine the countless song fragments he had collected into a single poetic work. He transposed oral tradition into a written language he had created himself. The tunes were of no interest to him. It was the text, the words, the great poem he wanted to highlight. In the course of the 1930s he amassed over four thousand verses, mostly two lines in length, which he edited and translated into English during the decade that followed.

But by 1950, the Aborigines of Australia were no longer the height of fashion in the European cultural world. Strehlow had trouble getting anyone even to flick through his manuscript. And those who did were startled by what they found. For most of the songs lacked any precise details about when, where and from whom they had been collected. And how reliable, in fact, were the transcripts that claimed to be 'condensed versions' of longer songs, or perhaps amalgamations of several different songs?

Instead of using accepted scientific techniques, Theo's book contained innumerable alleged parallels between the songs of the Arrernte people and western literature, from the medieval Icelandic *Hávamál* onwards. It was a monster of a book, which had to wait several decades before it was finally published, with a print run of just a thousand, in 1971.[134]

By then, most of the old singers were already dead. Theo felt himself to be the sole remaining custodian of a treasury of songs nobody remembered. And perhaps he himself had contributed to that loss of memory. Just as an actor remembers his lines by associating the words with particular movements and spatial positions, one of the roles of ritual is to act as a memory bank for the myths and songs of the people. Rite is a living national library in which poetry is enveloped and preserved through action. The poetry dies if it is separated from the rite.

The Arrernte people believed in a connection between cultural and biological survival. If the songs die, the land dies, if the ground dies, the people die. The old Arrernte men contemplated with horror a future in which their songs, rites and everything that kept the universe alive had sunk into oblivion.

This sense of doom permeates Theo Strehlow's entire life's work. His father at least had an alternative: God. Spencer believed in evolution, of which extinction was simply the inevitable reverse side. Strethlow had nothing but the bitterness of doom. His last words were: 'Oblivion that has no end.'[135]

88

In my dream I am lying on the ground under a tree. The crown of the tree is the memory of the Arrernte people. I see the brain stem disappearing into a huge mass of foliage. But the leaves begin to turn yellow, and in an autumnal storm of thoughts, they suddenly fall to the ground. This frightens me. But those that have fallen are the transient ones. In the remaining tracery of branches, new thoughts are alive; in fact when I look more closely, the twigs are already covered in buds.

89

A few years after Strehlow's death, the transistor radio created a new audience for the desert peoples' treasury of songs. In the 1970s and 80s, a hundred or so little radio stations sprang up. They became an important source of news and entertainment in the various Aboriginal languages, and mediated knowledge of those cultures.[136]

Radio proved in many ways to be the ideal medium for desert conditions. The technology is simple and cheap, the running costs are low. Newspapers and letters call for literacy and take a long time to reach the recipient. Radio builds on the spoken or sung word, which can reach the recipient the moment it is broadcast – or be saved for an audience scattered not only in space but also in time.

Production of audio cassettes developed into production of

video cassettes, which in turn led to the first illegal television broadcasts in Yuendumu in 1985. They were broadcasts of protest meetings, concerts and local sporting events. A speciality developed in personal greeting messages to distant kinsfolk. Face after face pops up on screen, greets Uncle This or Cousin That and asks if they are well. These programmes are tremendously popular – if the best thing you know is socializing with your relations, maybe the next best thing is seeing them on TV.

Other specialities include sand stories, documentary reports from holy places and food programmes about how to prepare grubs, seeds, roots and other traditional bush dishes. But above all the television broadcasts are facilitating a renaissance of traditional rites, dances and songs, enabled by the new technology to reach out to an audience many times greater than before. Songs which Strehlow believed sunk in oblivion with no end are now living on, on everybody's lips.

90

The Aborigines' pictures perplexed Australia's European 'discoverers' even more than their songs.

When early explorers found impressive cave paintings and rock carvings, they sometimes thought the images had been made not by the natives themselves but by some other, perhaps almost white race that had come in from outside, and that they thought they could glimpse among the blacks.[137]

But the more usual approach was to dismiss indigenous art as a kind of graffiti. As the German ethnologist Richard

Andree wrote in 1888 with reference to Australian rock art: 'If a drawing is done at a street corner, some imitator will soon come along and do another, and so school desks, outlook points and public toilets are soon filled with names and pictures.'[138]

Another German ethnologist, Erhard Eylmann, surmised that the strange patterns came about because it is easier to make lines and dots into some sort of pattern than to scatter them randomly over a surface. The natives' painting was a development of the make-up they used – the men paint themselves to be attractive to women. Eylmann himself favoured a different, more direct approach: 'It is my conviction that it would do most women good to receive a sound thrashing at least once a week.'[139]

Spencer and Gillen wanted clear and unambiguous indications from their informants of the significance of particular pictorial elements. It irritated them that a figure was said to be wholly without meaning when drawn in the sand, but assumed a very specific significance when it occurred on a holy object, and perhaps a different meaning again at a ceremonial site.[140]

But was this really so strange? Four numerals on a piece of paper might mean somebody was trying out their biro, but it could also be a date a schoolboy hopes to use for exam cheating, a code that opens locked doors, or even a PIN number allowing you to empty someone's bank account.

In their second book, Spencer and Gillen defined the pictorial elements as 'decorations' and regretted the fact that the natives often had no idea of their meaning. It didn't occur to them that their informants might have been keeping certain things secret to protect their bank accounts.

Ignorance hides behind condescending comments: 'Apparently, from the artistic point of view, the Central

George Grey discovered this cave painting in Kimberley and thought it must have been done by some other, almost white, race that had come in from outside, and that he imagined he could detect among the blacks.

Australian savage has been very little influenced by his natural surroundings, and delights in the production of wavy lines, circles and spirals . . .'[141]

Hardly an appropriate judgement of an art more deeply rooted in its local terrain than any other.

Even Spencer, an experienced map reader, can't see that the

circles and spirals of the 'savages' are a different, non-depictional way of reproducing the reality around them. Not even when he is at those locations does it occur to him that there are few objects in the desert that lend themselves to direct, realistic depiction. A central perspective generally only shows a small piece of ground which quickly disappears with distance, and a huge sky above the horizon. Flat ground looks like a mere line, unless viewed from above.[142]

The status of Aboriginal art in that period is perhaps most clearly illustrated in the Rautenstrauch-Joest Museum in Cologne. There, the hierarchy of the collections was built into the very building. Enthroned on the top floor were Asia, Africa and Indonesia. On the mezzanine below came the art of the more primitive American Indians. Another flight of stairs down: Melanesia, Polynesia and the rest of Oceania. On the ground floor: New Guinea. But the art from Australia, the continent in which 'the lowest forms of culture are preserved', was placed in the basement.[143]

91

'As in the tale of Sleeping Beauty, the Australian peoples have fallen asleep,' writes Herbert Kühn in *Die Kunst der Primitiven* (*The Art of the Primitives*, 1923). 'But for them, the prince of deliverance will never come, and they may not even wish to awaken from their slumber. Because for them, European culture implies not liberation but ruin.'[144]

But who in fact was sleeping and needed to be awoken? The black people or the white people?

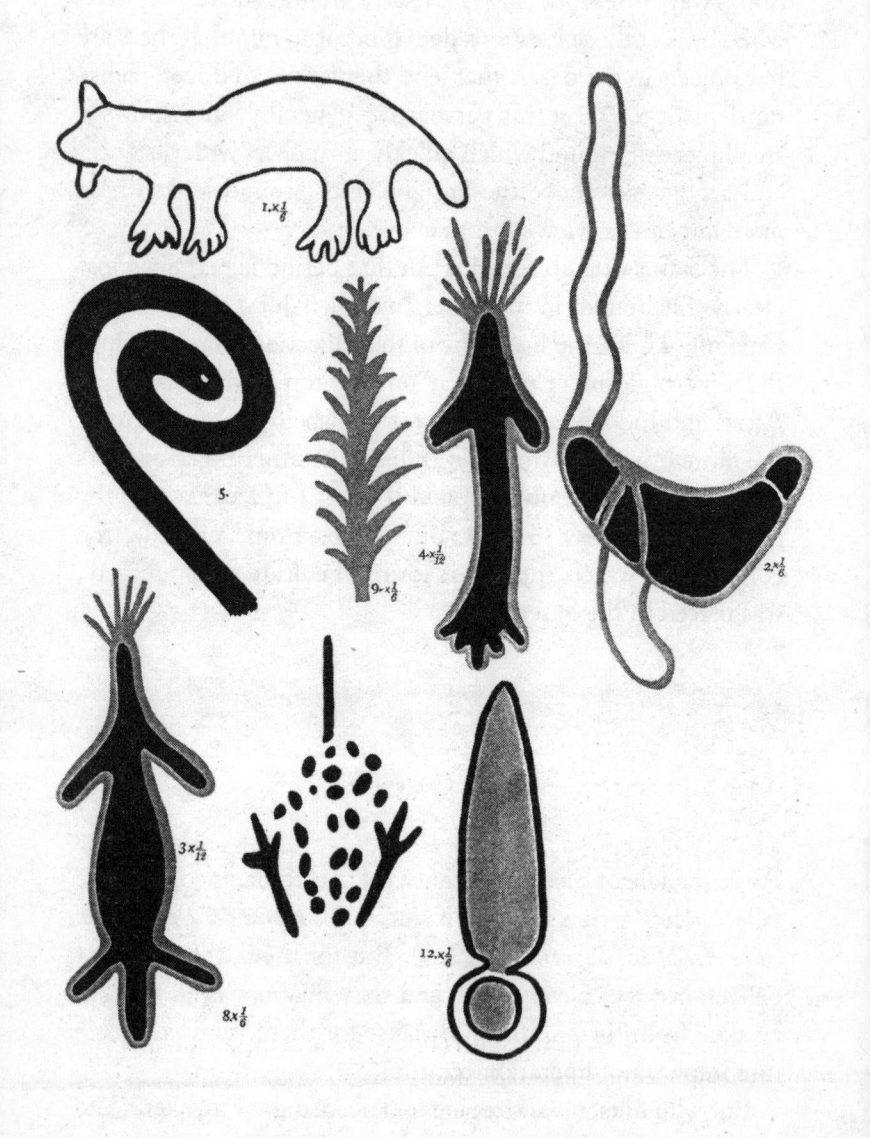

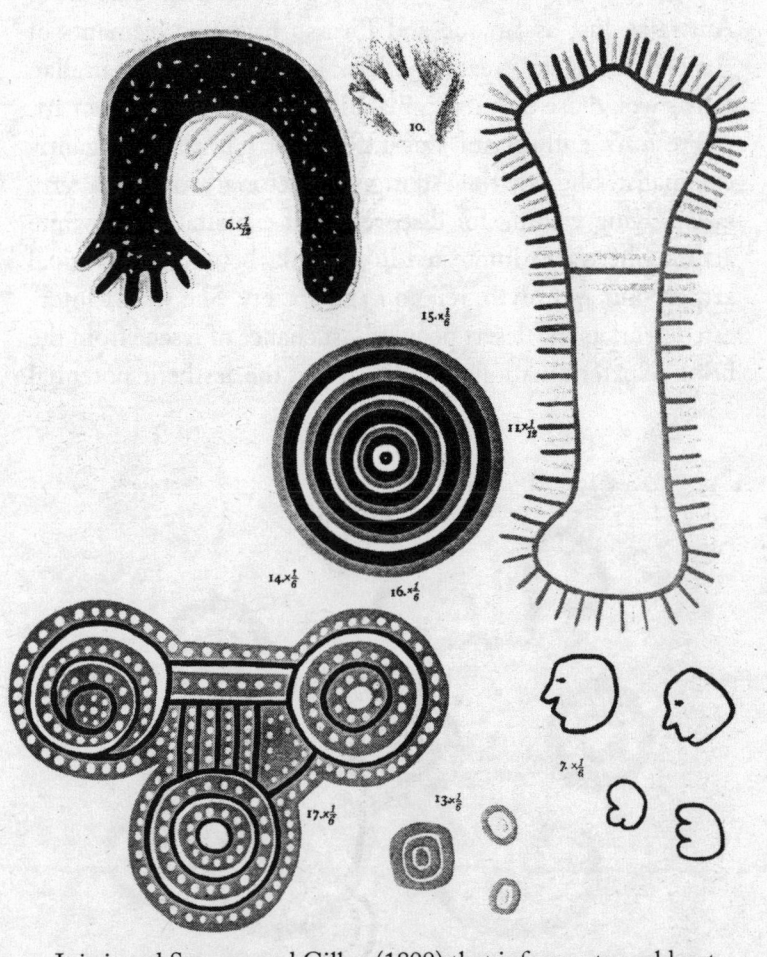

It irritated Spencer and Gillen (1899) that informants could not give clear and unambiguous information about the significance of the various elements of their pictures.

Margaret Preston was the first to wake up. She 'discovered' Aboriginal art in 1925 and was seized by a passionate belief that the whole set of native forms could be transposed into Western culture and be the starting point for a national art of Australia. Just as Braque and Picasso had used elements of African forms to create modern European art, Australian artists would use the Aboriginal idiom to renew their own art.

Preston's enthusiasm was infectious, but also arrogantly colonialist. She saw the Aborigines' pictorial world as a *terra nullius* lying waiting for discovery and exploitation by white artists. She wasn't interested in the links between Aboriginal art, ground and myth, religion and society. She wasn't interested in art as the desert peoples' last chance of rescue from the brink of extermination. She discovered the aesthetic potential

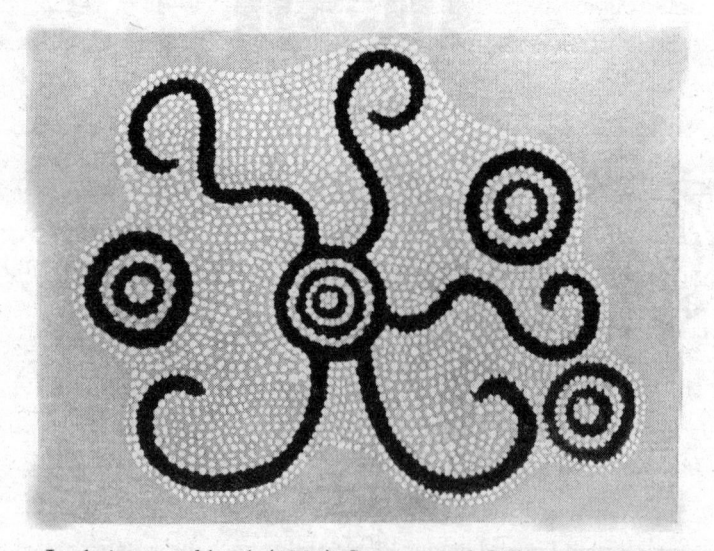

In their second book (1904), Spencer and Gillen classed the Aborigines' ground paintings as meaningless decoration.

of Aboriginal art, but saw it solely as an open treasure chest from which white artists could help themselves.[145]

92

Ten years later, Rex Battarbee woke up.[146] He was known for his watercolours, and often painted scenes from the area around Hermannsburg. His camel keeper, Albert, kept asking if he could learn to use watercolours. Within a few weeks, he was producing paintings virtually indistinguishable from those of the white artist. Battarbee took a couple and exhibited them in Melbourne. They sold within three days. A few years later, the National Art Gallery of South Australia acquired one of Albert Namatjira's watercolours. That was the first time a leading art gallery had bought work by an Aborigine.

Namatjira's work continued to sell well, and he was soon a prosperous man. Accustomed to sharing, he taught his techniques to his relatives, and before long all Hermannsburg was busy painting. A people that had been considered the world's artistically most impotent proved capable of unprecedented collective productivity in a branch of the arts that already had the full approval of the whites.

Albert Namatjira became the ultimate role model for the policy of assimilation. He was constantly held up as an example of how the Aborigine, by learning from the white man, could quickly become his cultural equal. No wonder Battarbee saw himself as the prince who had awoken Sleeping Beauty from her slumbers.

William Dargie, Australia 1921–2003, portrait of Albert Namatjira, 1956, oil on canvas, 102.1 × 76.4 cm, purchased 1957, collection of the Queensland Art Gallery.

In 1957, Namatjira's artistic achievements were rewarded with Australian citizenship. Namatjira was formally already an Australian citizen by virtue of the 1948 Nationality and Citizenship Act that ostensibly made all Australian Aborigines citizens – but citizens without the right to vote or any other civil rights.[147]

In 1948 the Aborigines of the Alice Springs area could still be interned against their will; they were not allowed into white hotels, hospitals or other 'prohibited areas' and could not travel or leave employment without permission. They were outside the social security system and did not receive old age pensions, maternity allowances or any other social benefits. Marriages were prohibited across racial boundaries, except by special permission from the authorities.

The 1953 Welfare Ordinance (NT) replaced all earlier Aboriginal Ordinances and substituted the word 'ward' for 'Aborigine'. The criteria for being declared a 'ward' were ostensibly racially neutral. They included lifestyle, behaviour and personal associations. According to these criteria more than 99 per cent of the Aboriginal population were declared 'wards' of the state.

In 1959 the Director of Welfare decided to prohibit marriage between Mick Daly (white) and Gladys Namagu (black). The incident attracted international attention and after the intervention of the UN Secretary-General, the Director changed his decision. The global decolonization process had made the racial laws of Australia increasingly conspicuous, and the government came under considerable international pressure to change the rules.

In 1962 Aboriginal people acquired the right to vote in both state and Commonwealth elections. Two years later the concept of 'ward' was abolished and the Aborigines became 'persons who in the opinion of the Director are socially or economically in need of assistance'. The change in terms changed little in the authorities' practice of power. In 1966 Aboriginal people were included in the Australian social system. Their social benefits however, were often not paid out to them personally, but to their employer or to the institution in which they were confined.

Finally, in a 1967 referendum, 90 per cent of Australians voted 'yes' to changing the Constitution in order to include Aboriginal people in the national census. The referendum had great symbolic significance, but the fight for full citizenship rights went on well into the 1980s.

Under this protracted process, what did 'citizenship' mean in Namatjira's case?

When the 1953 Welfare Ordinance came into operation in 1957, Namatjira was not on the list of Aborigines declared 'wards of the state'. This meant that he could vote, be served in restaurants and treated in hospitals reserved for white people. He was free from all restrictions governing the life of 'wards'.

In Alice Springs, many thought this was too great an honour for a 'black ape'. Namatjira came under intense small-town scrutiny.

Did he have his children with him after dark? He wasn't allowed to do that, because only Australian citizens were allowed to be in Alice in the evenings, and Albert's children weren't citizens. Had he been drinking with his relations? He wasn't allowed to do that, because offering Aborigines alcohol was prohibited.

Of course, innumerable white people broke these rules and went unpunished. They earned good money illicitly supplying alcohol to black people, and kept their black mistresses in their beds well after nightfall. But when the police caught Namatjira and a fellow family member drunk in a taxi, the full force of the law was brought to bear. The local court sentenced Namatjira to six months' hard labour for supplying his relative with intoxicating beverages.

Taking account of the criminal's age and failing health, a superior court reduced his sentence to three months. The Supreme Court in Canberra confirmed the sentence on 12 March 1959. The local correspondent of *The News* got the first comment from a shattered Namatjira: 'Why don't they kill us all? That is what they want.'[148]

He was taken to the internment camp at Papunya, two hundred kilometres north-west of Alice Springs, where he was kept isolated from the other inmates. But naturally they still drew their conclusions. Assimilation, even at its most successful, could only ever end in humiliation and disaster.

Albert Namatjira served his sentence, and died of a heart attack soon after his release. After two years as an Australian citizen, he was buried on 9 August 1959.

94

Those ethnologists who first took an interest in Aboriginal images in the 1930s made quick forays into the desert, handed out brown paper and chalks, collected in the drawings and the explanations of them, and then sat down to count up the different elements of form. The collection method was one-sided, the analysis superficial.[149]

The first person to study the desert peoples' imagery in depth was the American researcher Nancy D. Munn. She came to Yuendumu in 1956 and remained with the Warlpiri people for over a year. She was interested in the links between images and dreams, between songs and tracks.

Songs and tracks arose simultaneously in the dreams of the Warlpiri's ancestors. They dreamed their tracks. When they woke up, they gave material form to their dream by singing the song and drawing the track. As they were travelling, they sang their journey; they sang the names of the places and the song for each place; they sang about their journey and events along the way. And these events left their tracks in landscape as well as in song. The whole desert became a statement of their ancestors' dreams and exploits.

The structure of the travelogue binds action, dream and song to specific places in space – actual, existing places that can be visited even when the dreamer is awake. Since all the ancestors are linked to specific places, they can be represented by pictures of these places. The ancestors have left their traces at these locations, and that's not all: the place *is* the trace. The place would not exist and be as it is, if the ancestor had not arrived there and left the place behind as a trace of his or her visit. The land the whites called *terra nullius* was the ancestors' work, and it was the task of the living to maintain it.[150]

Some songs, Nancy D. Munn writes, consist exclusively of place names, and the word for song itself, *yiri*, also means 'name', 'visible mark' or 'trace'. The Warlpiri people call a series of songs a 'songline', and it is an exact equivalent of a series of places that exist in the real world.

It was these 'songlines' that were made famous a quarter of a century later by Bruce Chatwin's book of the same name.

95

The scholars up to that point, all men, had been interested predominantly in the men's pictures, particularly the secret pictures that only men were allowed to see. Nancy Munn, on the other hand, ignored the high-status ceremonies of the men and approached things from a different direction. She observed the variations in the way the two sexes used pictures.

Warlpiri of both sexes draw in the sand when they are telling stories or arguing. But not in the same way. The men seem to put an overhead projector picture down in the sand at intervals, as if to illustrate some specific point in their presentation. The picture is used as a store-room for knowledge that also exists in other forms. The picture can be unrolled verbally and the words can then be rolled back up into a picture. Women, by contrast, draw a whole stream of pictures, what Munn terms 'a continuous running graphic notation'. The Warlpiri women have made storytelling to the accompaniment of pictures into a unique art form: *djugurba*, the sand story.[151]

A sand story consists of rhythmically hummed words and accompanying gestures which explain the essence of the story: a sort of manual choreography in the sand. The movements of the hand as it shapes the pictures are what represent the action of the story. The ground itself 'has' the story, the hand merely performs it in the sand, before the ground reclaims it.

'And they all lived happily ever after.' That's how our traditional stories end. But the Warlpiri's sand stories end with everybody disappearing into the sand. The female storyteller draws a circle and makes all her characters enter it and go down into the ground. The words she says as they vanish are always the same: *Lawa-djari-dja-lgu*, 'And so they became nothing.'

Most Warlpiri women have a wide repertoire of such stories, which they perform using mime, voice, gestures and signs in the sand. Any little girl of about eight or nine can make up a sand story and bring it to life. She tells it to other girls or younger boys. An older boy, however, won't listen to sand stories because they are part of the female role.

Tracks left by animals and people are common in sand stories. The tracks are made with the hand, which is held in different positions to produce the prints left by birds, animals and people. Making hand tracks like these is a game adults often play with children. The art of tracking animal prey is naturally vital for the desert folk's traditional food supply. But

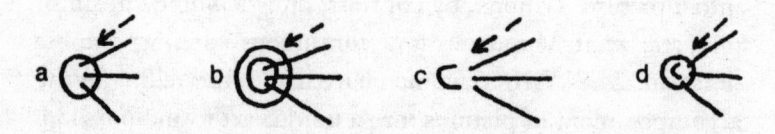

The Warlpiri people's sand stories end with everyone disappearing into the sand. The female storyteller draws a circle and makes all her characters enter it and go down into the ground, with the words *'Lawa-djari-dja-lgu,'* 'And so they became nothing.' Illustration from Munn, *Walbiri Iconography*.

more important still are footsteps and other things a body may leave behind, as intersections between human being and ground.

The ground is the desert people's religion. A footprint in the sand is the key to their imagery.

96

Marcel Réja is the first, and most overlooked, theoretician of modern art.

If anybody remembers him today, it's for being nice to August Strindberg. They met in Paris in 1897. Strindberg was out to conquer Paris and wrote a novel in French, *Inferno*. Réja helped him, wrote a preface for the book and arranged for it to be published by his own publishing house, Mercure de France.

The pseudonym Marcel Réja concealed a young doctor, Paul Gaston Meunier, who a few years later received his PhD for a dissertation on psychiatry. Under his own name he wrote a thick book on the interpretation of dreams: *Les Rêves et leur interprétation* (*Dreams and their Interpretation*, 1910).

But Marcel Réja's most creative contribution to scholarship was the book *L'Art chez les fous* (*The Art of the Mentally Deranged*, 1907). The book was published in two editions the same year Picasso painted 'Les Desmoiselles d'Avignon'. Among the twenty-six illustrations there are many that anticipate Picasso, such as a child's drawing of a face seen simultaneously from the front and the side.

Réja links the art of the mentally ill with children's drawings and the fetishes of 'savages', and finds in these three forms of expression a primitive originality and power that were lacking in the conventional art of the period. He refers to the pictures as 'ideogrammatic scripts', calling them 'hieroglyphic drawings that express their ideas through bold distortions'.

An African fetish 'has no need to be beautiful'; it lacks 'the seduction of art'. A crudely carved idol from the Niger River gives a highly simplified idea of the human face: three cylinders of different sizes placed one on top of the other, one forming the forehead, another the nose, a third the rest of the face. The fetish represents the human being in 'toute sa nudité géométrique', all its geometric nakedness.

By the Ogooué River in Gabon, Marcel Réja writes, we find a number of geometric works in which simplicity has been taken to its limits. The face is depicted with wilful simplification as a flat surface with only the nose protruding. Interpreting this as proof of incompetence would be unjust. This is a different kind of art, an art that scorns representation and seeks to reproduce, not the outward form of reality, but its concept.

'Reduction to the geometrically abstract however remains the general principle of all this art,' concludes Réja – thereby providing the formula which Picasso and Braque set about putting into practice in the first Cubist paintings a few months later, opening the door to the modern era in Western art.

The artists reacted immediately, but it took half a century for Réja's ideas to filter through to public consciousness.

In the vanguard was the Museum of Modern Art in New York, which mounted exhibitions of African art in 1935, of

Mexican in 1940, Native American in 1941, South Pacific art in 1946, and more African art in 1953. In 1957 the Museum of Primitive Art in New York opened, and in 1971 the decision was taken to move the collections to a new wing of the Metropolitan Museum of Art. Thus 'primitive' art became firmly anchored in the world's most exclusive museum environment.[152]

97

But Australia still wasn't represented. Why?

There's a mutual connection between 'art' and 'collecting art', wrote Shelly Errington in 1998. 'Art' has to exist in order for people to collect it, and if no one collects it, then it isn't 'art'.

For artefacts to be collected, they have to be permanent and portable. The Aborigines' ground paintings could be neither preserved nor transported. They were danced down into the ground. Body paintings washed off or wore away. The drawings of the sand stories disappeared into the sand. They were all part of a combined art form in which the picture was incomplete without story, song and dance. They were all components of unique happenings that would never happen in exactly the same way again.

In order to become 'art', the picture had to be lifted out of this context, lifted from the ground and the skin and attached to a new backing, made permanent and cut into rectangular pieces that could be demarcated from their surroundings in frames.

Packaged like this, the picture could be sold on a market and become part of a collection. Cut out like this, it could demand entry into new contexts, such as the Metropolitan Museum in New York and art galleries in other cities round the world.

It took something as radical as a Caesarean section, but only that one, single cut, to make the inhabitants of the Australian deserts once again the best-known, the most interesting and most debated indigenous peoples in the world.

98

At the end of the nineteenth century, Spencer and Gillen saw themselves as the 'discoverers' of the Arrernte people. It has subsequently become clear that the Arrernte people consciously selected Gillen, to try to break through the wall of white incomprehension. Theo Strehlow likewise saw himself as the Homer of the Arrernte people. But it was the Arrernte who entrusted him with their treasury of songs. And it was Namatjira who actively persuaded Battarbee, not the other way round.

Namatjira had shown that Aborigines, too, could create Western art. Margaret Preston had shown that Aboriginal art, too, could inspire Western artists. The questions remained: why did the idiom of the blacks only become art when imitated by white artists? Why did the Aborigines become artists only when they imitated the art of the whites?

It was in Papunya, Namatjira's place of detention, that the answer to these questions suddenly became evident.

Papunya was the jewel in the crown of the little gulag of native internment camps set up to implement the policy of assimilation.[153] There, the Aborigines were to learn to live settled lives in corrugated-iron huts, in nameless, symmetrical rows of streets. They were to learn to keep to times, to dress respectably and blow their noses in handkerchiefs.

The department had patrols out in the desert, which rounded up small groups of nomads and herded them to Lajamanu, Yuendumu or Papunya, where they were kept while their culture was soaked off them, like removing paint from old wooden furniture with lye. The result was apathy, intense homesickness and a feverish interest in their own culture.

One day, a new schoolteacher arrived. He said hello to everyone he met, even black people. This caused amazement.

The new teacher took his food and went to sit in the black section of the dining hall. No one had ever done that before.

The new teacher, Geoffrey Bardon, had a small grant to look into the possibility of making cartoons in the style of Aboriginal art. He needed to know how the shapes would look when enlarged on to the big screen. He and his interpreter painted a few clumsy Aborigine motifs on a wall in an odd corner of the school.

The school caretakers, Bill Stockman and Long Jack, saw at once that this was something they could do much better than the teacher. Could they join in and help? Of course! More and more walls in the school were decorated with paintings, more and more of the respected old men took an interest: Old Tom Onion, Old Mick, Old Walter, Old Bert, Old Tutuma.

Terra Nullius

This happened in the period May–August 1971. First the small surfaces were covered with paintings; eventually only the large ones were left to do. The grand finale was a painting ten metres by three, which dominated the whole school and its surroundings. It made a powerful impression, firstly because of its shameless size, secondly because it set an Aboriginal stamp on a European building.

Filling the wall with 'The Dream of the Honeybee' was an audacious challenge to the camp's programme of indoctrination, and emphatically announced: 'We've got our own culture. And we intend to hang on to it.'

100

Tensions in Papunya had led to rioting and damage on several previous occasions. Now the men had found a way amidst all the degradation of the camp to recreate something of what had made their lives in the desert meaningful. Soon they were queuing up to get brushes and acrylic paints from Bardon.

When the school walls were all used up, they found new things to paint on: worn old linoleum boards from the staff accommodation blocks (they had just been replaced by new ones and left lying outside the buildings).

Linoleum boards were something usually seen from above, and walked on, like the ground. The boards were a kind of ground, but transportable. The boards turned out to be saleable ground, too. Bardon took some of them to Alice and got almost $100 each for them. The following weekend, boards were

190

sold for a total of $1,300. It caused a sensation in Papunya, where money of your own meant a dramatic increase in personal freedom.

In the months that followed, there were at least five large cash transactions involving six hundred paintings by twenty-five different artists. The internees were already starting to dream of buying an old car to visit their former homelands in the desert.

Was it a coincidence that the desert happened to bloom that year, 1971? After several years of drought, the rains finally came. They not only filled the usual waterholes and underground streams, but also flowed across the land in rivers tens of kilometres wide. Nature burst its banks and gave its human inhabitants the courage to do the same.

The camp authorities lost control of the workforce and were furious. They refused to pay out the usual 'training allowance' if the men didn't chop wood. What they had earned from their art would be confiscated for the Crown. The camp director came to the painting room and announced that the art was 'government property'. Government 'expenses' would be subtracted from the latest sales profit of $700, leaving the remaining $21 to be divided between the artists as a bonus for diligence.

When Bardon entered the painting room, forty accusing faces met his gaze. The expectations he had aroused had proved unrealistic. Paints and brushes were thrown down into the sand; nobody would paint without payment. They all chanted in unison, 'Money, money, money . . .'

Bardon writes: 'I was finished, truly finished, I knew; and I drove out of Papunya in July 1972 with a despair and a fury I had never known before, towards Alice Springs, for I had truly lost the game.'[154]

At that point, the Geoffrey Bardon episode could have run into the sand like so many other sand stories. That was the fate of Noel White and his wife in Carrolup in the 1940s, and of various others who tried: 'And so they became nothing.'

But in 1972, the situation was rather different. A Labor government with new Aborigine policies came to power at the end of the year. The aim was no longer to eradicate native cultures, but to highlight and preserve them. The Aboriginal Arts Board was set up, with the task of supporting and encouraging artistic initiatives. A series of successors to Bardon dealt with the finances, organized exhibitions and marketed Papunya art.

Local opposition was still fierce. While the Papunya painters were holding a highly acclaimed exhibition in Sydney in 1974, the camp authorities seized their chance and white-washed over the offending murals on the walls of the school.

Even within Aboriginal society there was some opposition. It was felt that the artists were selling the secrets of their people and trading in holy symbols. The criticism led to a gradual disappearance of ritually 'dangerous' motifs. The ethno-logical content of the art was watered down. Traditional forms were used in a much freer, more personal way.

When the first wave of enthusiasm had died down, opposi-tion also hardened among white art critics. What was this they were being asked to admire? A two-headed calf – one head in the Stone Age, the other in Modernism? It couldn't be con-sidered anything but a transient curiosity. 'Curiosity art', it was dubbed. 'Souvenir art'. 'Tourist art'.

And naturally not all the thousands of paintings produced

in Papunya were epoch-making. Most of what gets painted is rubbish, even in Paris or New York. The remarkable thing was rather that a small place with only 1,500 inhabitants, living in total isolation from the rest of the art world, could produce twenty or more great artists.

The breakthrough came in 1980, when the National Art Gallery in Canberra bought their first acrylic painted by an Aboriginal artist. In the same year, a large private collector bought some hundred works by the leading Papunya artists. Perhaps even more significantly, the South Australian Museum bought Clifford Possum's 'Man's Love Story' and hung it not in ethnic isolation but along with work by other contemporary modern artists.[155] The painting immediately dominated the huge room, making all the other artwork nearby seem anxiously insignificant.

The international breakthrough came ten years later, as the *Dreamings* exhibition toured New York, Chicago and Los Angeles in 1988–1990.[156] It was now quite clear that the Papunya artists were not mining some little ethnological deposit that would soon be exhausted. No, this was a group of independent artists, each developing in their own way from a common starting point.

102

I met Geoffrey Bardon in his home in Taree, on the east coast of Australia. Sadly, I was too late. The cancer already had him in its grip. He could only say a few words. A couple of weeks later, he was dead.

'How did you come to get interested in the Aborigines?' I ask.

'Geoff wasn't particularly interested in Aborigines until he got to Papunya,' says his wife, Dawn.

As she speaks, Geoff is summoning up the strength to answer:

'I met some severely oppressed human beings.'

And he adds: 'The nurse in Papunya said, "They come here healthy. After three weeks they're all sick."'

And a while later: 'I've always been for the underdog.'

Now he was death's underdog. He knew it, he said it, and his eyes often dulled. He was slipping away. But before he disappeared, he was intensely present in his look, still shining with the fire of the miracle in Papunya.

'What pictures did you bring with you to Papunya? What did you show them? Picasso? Klee?'

'I didn't have any pictures. I read poetry. I had poems.'

'Which poems?'

'The Spanish poets. Lorca, above all.'

Tall trees and birdsong. A cockatoo chatters in its cage, a dog barks at the back of the house. Geoff is sitting with his eyes closed and seems to have fallen asleep. But suddenly his eyelids open and his gaze is clear and straight.

It's my own gaze that flinches from the solemn truth of death. At the edge of my field of vision I see a Turner reproduction and some watercolours. I get up and take a closer look. They're Bardon's own watercolours from his years in Papunya. Sensitive, but conventional. And above all horizontal, in fact almost exclusively horizon – as the desert is, until you start seeing it from above.

Amazing! So this was how Bardon was perceiving the world, while a totally different reality was breaking through in

Papunya. The art he was encouraging was the polar opposite of the one he practised himself.

Geoffrey Bardon wasn't one of the 'Bardon Men', as the Papunya painters were called. Artistically, where subject matter and technique were concerned, he was still in Hermannsburg. Like White in Carrolup, he himself would never have been able to produce the pictures that were being created in Papunya. It wasn't a case of Bardon showing the Aborigines what to do.

103

'I didn't have any pictures. I had poems,' Geoffrey Bardon said. I wonder if he'd read Theo Strehlow's *The Songs*, which was published in 1971, just when it was all happening in Papunya.

Both Strehlow and Bardon won the confidence of the desert peoples. Both were destined to be instruments in the survival of the desert peoples. They did the same thing in opposite ways.

In 1971, the Aborigines of Central Australia had neither 'art' nor 'poetry' as we understand them. They had ceremonies in which body-painting and ground-painting were bound up with dance, music and song.

Strehlow took away everything except the words of the songs, the words as written down by him, presumably coloured by his own Lutheran emotionalism. Strehlow distilled the 'poetry' from the rite.

Geoffrey Bardon took away everything except the picture, the picture as he pulled it free and enlarged it on to walls, and presumably coloured by his own knowledge of modern, abstract art. Bardon distilled the 'art' from the rite – and the Bardon Men immediately seized the opportunity that this created.

Strehlow made printable text in written language out of the ritual songs. The Bardon Men made permanent, portable acrylic paintings out of the ritual body and ground paintings.

The difference was that Strehlow exercised complete control over the text, and vainly attempted to control its interpretation, too. Bardon, by contrast, gave full rein to creative chaos.

The result was that the acrylics found a market, something the texts without tunes failed to achieve. The acrylics were constantly developing new painters, whereas the text could not liberate new poets or theatre. Strehlow's project was a one-man business. Bardon created a popular movement that spread all over the deserts of central Australia.

104

In Yuendumu, horror mingled with delight as they observed the new route to respect and income opening up in their sister colony, Papunya.[157] The menfolk were afraid the ritual secrets on which their power rested would be revealed. The women of Yuenduma had no such secrets. Their sand stories belonged to anyone and everyone. Their ceremonies were open. For them, the step from rite to art was a shorter one.

The initiative came from a circle of ritually active women who routinely met early in the mornings to narrate and discuss their dreams. This group decided in 1984 to follow Papunya's example. The aim was to buy a Toyota to bring the holy places of their people within reach. Economic and religious objectives were from the outset closely intertwined.[158]

Just as in Papunya, their pictures were of the ground. Or rather, the history of the ground. A geologist sees the land-scape as the result of historic and prehistoric processes: the Pre-Cambrian rock has been folded, faultlines have opened, sediment has built up. Events that have been in progress for hundreds of millions of years lie exposed in the present moment. The landscape carries with it the narrative of its cre-ation. In a similar way, the ground speaks to the Aborigines of a permanently present mythical history, which shapes their lives and society.

In rite, you painted the ground. In art, you painted images of the ground. The images were designed to be seen from above, any way up. They were made not for the wall but for the floor, or rather for the ground, themselves a sort of concen-trated ground, a surface removable from the ground.

The women who were leaders in the rite also became lead-ers in the art movement. Only they had the capacity to mobilize the collaboration that supports both rite and art. Even if there is a single name at the bottom of the picture, most works of art are the result of collaboration. Someone has shared their knowledge, someone has done the actual painting, others have made adjustments and additions. All those who played a part have a right to remuneration, so the price of the artwork is distributed within the kinship group. Since they are building on the knowledge of the elders and need their approval, the elders' position is strengthened. In Yuendumu it was predominantly the women's position that was boosted, because the initiative had been theirs.

A few months later it was the men's turn. In Papunya, the

Dorothy Napangardi with winning work 'Salt on Mina Mina',
synthetic polymer paint on linen, 2001, 244 × 168 cm, at the
18th Telstra National Aboriginal and Torres Strait Islander
Art Award 2001. Courtesy of the Museum and
Art Gallery of the Northern Territory.

men had painted the school walls; in Yuendumu they painted the school doors. Yuendumu had waited twelve years. Now, thirty-six doors were painted in one go. The men painted with the audacious speed of graffiti artists, with broad brushes, big brush-strokes and vibrant colours. The result was a concentrate of the desert people's wealth of myths, assembled in one place, captured in a single moment: the quintessence of a culture.

105

The 1980s saw the art movement spreading like wildfire from Papunya and Yuendumu to the other desert settlements: Kintore in 1981, Kiwirkurra in 1983, Balgo in 1985, Lajamanu in 1986, Utopia in 1987. Both men and women were involved, and altogether over a thousand new desert artists were painting. Their work was analysed and discussed in a flood of art books all over the world.

Once Papunya had broken the ice, the other groups soon gained entry to the big museums. In Darwin I heard white people going sceptically round the galleries. Art? This? Twenty years ago these were just the darkies' doodlings!

But the prices speak a language even the whites in Darwin must understand. Paintings that once sold for a hundred now cost hundreds of thousands of dollars. A high point was reached in 2001, when a painting by Rover Thomas was sold for over three-quarters of a million dollars.[159]

Today there is a score of painting communities in the desert. Many of the artists are old women who have never even been in Alice Springs. Most of them don't speak English. But their pictures reach the whole world via satellite. They exhibit in Tokyo and New York.

106

Is there any other example of a whole people turning to art as a route to liberation?

Inuits and Aborigines were 'discovered' about the same time. Edward Nelson's standard work *The Eskimo* (1899) came out the same year as Spencer and Gillen's *The Native Tribes of Central Australia*. Fifty years later, Canadian James Houston saw the artistic potential of Eskimo sculpture and created a market for it – just as Geoffrey Bardon, a quarter of a century after that, would find a market for Aboriginal art.

By the time another twenty-five years had passed, the Aborigines and Inuit were internationally acknowledged, and above all as artists. Art was their major export, and there were villages in which nearly 80 per cent of the adult population earned their living as artists.

Such concentration of artistic talent in just two peoples ought not to be possible – if we assume talent is distributed fairly equally across humanity. But perhaps that assumption of equal distribution is too hasty? Hot springs and volcanic activity aren't distributed evenly across the earth's crust, so why should creativity be?

Perhaps eruptions of creativity are associated not so much with peoples as with particular situations in history? When Picasso brought the African and European traditions together in 'Les Demoiselles d'Avignon', he opened the floodgates of creative force, not just among his own people but spanning his whole age. A new way of painting prompted a new way of looking at and defining art, which in turn broadened the spectrum of artistic talent that could win acclaim.

In the final analysis, maybe it's the assumption of the rarity of artistic talent we should be questioning? In my day, the accepted view was that only a few scholarly pupils would benefit from higher education. Today, most young people go on to university or further study.

Both the Inuit and the Aborigines live in extremely inhospitable terrain in extremely harsh climatic conditions. Both have had their conception of the world and their lifestyle demolished. Both have repeatedly been declared doomed to extinction. Both have high death rates from illness, drug use, depression and suicide. Art is often their only salvation. Art is none the worse for coming from the very brink of the abyss.

Both Inuit and Aborigine traditionally lived in cultures without any division of labour other than that between the sexes. All the men were expected to be able to hunt; all the women were expected to be able to find roots or prepare sealskins. Everyone was expected to be capable of doing everything, within the traditional sex roles. Art was no exception. There was an underlying assumption that anybody could produce art if they just knuckled down to it.

Both cultures have a tradition of everyone taking part. All the Warlpiri women tell sand stories to their children; all the Inuit women practise 'story-knifing', in which the plot is drawn with a knife on the frozen crust of the snow. All Inuit men help to bring down their quarry when hunting; they all draw their ancestors' exploits in blood from their own noses. All Aboriginal men paint the ground and their bodies, celebrate in song their ancestors' feats and play their part in maintaining the world order. Everyone can take part in the holy rites − so why shouldn't they take part, too, when the images detach themselves from the rite and become what we call art?

If one of us can, everyone can. On that basis, it turns out that whole villages can produce superb works of art which win them acclaim from the world and raise them out of misery and dependence.

107

When Bardon arrived at Papunya in 1971, the Aborigines' history was as unknown as their art.

The fiction of Australia as a *terra nullius* demanded a mental suppression of the Aborigines. White historians wrote nothing of the Aborigines' achievements, or even of their existence. In white historiography, the Aborigines long remained an inferior race doomed to 'fade away' on contact with Western culture.[161]

There was no investigation of the violence that precipitated this 'fading'. Historians spoke of violence in general terms, without concrete examples. '[This] mental block has by no means disappeared,' wrote C. D. Rowley in *The Destruction of Aboriginal Society* (1970−1), a pioneering work which tried for the first time to see Australian history from an Aboriginal point of view.

Rowley shows that the living conditions imposed on the Aborigines actually meant it was far easier for them to die than adapt to the new circumstances. 'White consciences were salved by romanticizing high death rates as a graceful making way for the higher race in the inevitable contest for survival.'[162]

'Those involved in their killing naturally enough were ready to equate them with forms of life less than human,' Rowley wrote. Those Aborigines who survived in the remnants of a defeated society lived in a hopelessness and apathy that seemed to confirm the settlers' worst prejudices.[163]

In some parts of the Australian outback, those prejudices are still very much alive. But in modern Australia, in Sydney, Melbourne and other cities an educated minority questions the old attitudes. People are recognizing that the only Australian culture that time and again has made an international impact is Aborigine culture. They are recognizing that this supposedly doomed ethnic group is actually displaying exceptional powers of survival. Contempt gives way to admiration as they see the consistency with which the Aborigines have held fast to the foundations of their traditional culture, and the flexibility with which they have been able to adapt it to modern technology and modern society.

The question is: how will the new Australia face up to the crimes committed by the old one, the effects of which are still having a major impact on the living conditions of the Aborigines? How will modern-day Australia come to terms with its past?

The perpetrators in the majority of cases can no longer be put on trial. By which laws would they be judged? How can the dead be punished? Neither perpetrators nor victims can live their lives over again. It's the survivors who've got to devise a new way of dealing with the after-effects of the crimes.

One very important aspect of this is the distribution of land – that land which is so fundamental to the desert peoples' economic, social and ritual lives.

It's a problem not just in Australia but in many other

countries, Sweden among them. ILO Convention 107, Article 2, establishes the duty of all states to acknowledge 'the right of ownership, collective or individual, of the members of [indigenous] populations concerned over the lands which these populations traditionally occupy'. Sweden, which doesn't want to acknowledge the injustice done to the Sami, has refused to ratify the Convention.[164] Australia, which does not want to acknowledge the injustice done to the Aborigines, has not signed either.

108

Three hundred million human beings on this planet are members of indigenous peoples who have been, or are on the way to being, robbed of their land. They are generally among the poorest and most scorned minorities in the countries where they live. Not long ago, they were considered doomed to die out. But in recent decades, the indigenous peoples have seized back the initiative on a global scale.

July 1990 saw the first Continental Indigenous International Convention, held in Quito. There were four hundred delegates from 120 nations. The meeting was hosted by one of the most active movements in South America, the Confederation of Indigenous Nationalities of Ecuador, which considers itself to represent 30 per cent of its country's population. The Convention's central demands concern land and education. The overarching vision is to gather the indigenous peoples into a new, trans-border, 'multinational nation'.

The Ground

In Australia, less than a generation ago, white civil servants were busy stripping the Aborigines of their original culture, while other white civil servants had the task of trying to 'save' the remains of a dying people. They were all caught equally unawares by the artistic vitality that suddenly came bubbling up from this culturally devastated land. The artistic renaissance went hand in hand with a political and legal reappraisal.

Australia began a decade-long process of reconciliation between white and black by declaring 1991 the Year of the Indigenous Peoples. Prime Minister Keating inaugurated the year with the words: 'It was we who did the dispossessing. We committed the murders. We took the children from their mothers. We practised discrimination and exclusion.'[165]

On 3 June 1992, the Australian High Court outlawed the concept of '*terra nullius*' and ratified Aboriginal rights to the land where they lived, and had always lived. The so-called Mabo Decision revised the whole historic and legal basis of Australia as a nation.

But in 1996, Labor was voted out of power, partly for its pro-Aboriginal rights policy. Then the Aborigines felt the impact of swingeing budget cuts. In the new political climate, even the Mabo decision proved to be worth less than initially hoped. The new government countered the decision with amendments to the Native Title Act, preventing claims over large tracts of pastoral and mining land. In order to make a claim, the Aborigines have to show a continuing connection to the land. Since most of them have been robbed of their land, or forced into cities and towns by unemployment, or abducted from their parents as children, many have lost the right to the lands of their fathers.

Australian race relations have become a major theme in both academic research and popular accounts of the country's history. This disturbs many white Australians. They used to see themselves as peaceful and law-abiding settlers, who had brought the blessings of civilization to the indigenous inhabitants of Australia. They are understandably reluctant to let historical research rob them of this beautiful picture and substitute a history of mass killing, land-theft, rape, kidnapping and other outrages. Many prefer to turn a blind eye to the growing mountain of evidence of their forefathers' violence and racism.

Others go on the offensive and scrutinize the evidence for mistakes. Never have historians had their footnotes so closely perused as in contemporary Australia. A missing comma here, a misspelt name or a wrong date there – in hundreds of scholarly publications there are bound to be some mistakes and the attackers use them to discredit the whole profession.

Foremost among the attackers is Keith Windschuttle. According to his *The Fabrication of Aboriginal History, vol 1* (2002) no genocide was committed, the massacres were legitimate police actions and there was no reign of terror based on widespread violence. Windschuttle rejects practically everything academic historians have found out about Aboriginal history during the last thirty-five years. It is all a gigantic forgery, intended to deprive Australians of the right to be proud of their history.

Another revisionist, Michael Connor, maintains that Australia as a nation was not founded on the fiction that the land was empty and belonged to no one, or at least to no one who wasn't doomed to extinction. In *The Invention of Terra Nullius* (2005) he alleges that the *terra nullius* doctrine was created in the 1970s by a conspiracy of politicized historians and ignorant judges.

The tone is astonishingly vituperative. Every argument is accompanied by an insult. According to the attackers, when professional historians started to research Aboriginal history in the 1970s, they were suddenly transformed into bitter academics, frozen moralists, power-hungry careerists, self-flattering elitists and latte-stained conformists. They were said to gag history and torture their sources in order to produce trendy results, applauded by corrupt colleagues lobotomizing themselves in public.

The goal of the revisionists, in the words of Prime Minister John Howard, is to make Australians 'comfortable and relaxed about their history'. Their method is denial. They deny the obvious fact that before the British arrival the country belonged to the indigenous population. They deny that the Aborigines resisted British occupation. They deny that settlers killed large numbers of Aborigines on the frontier and terrified others to submission. They deny the role the British invasion played in the catastrophe that annihilated some nine-tenths of the Aboriginal population, extinguishing several hundred peoples, each with its own language and culture.[166]

110

'History', said I. A. Richards, 'is simply a record of things which ought not to have happened.'[167]

Recent decades have seen the history of élites being increasingly replaced by the history of ordinary peoples. When the rich and victorious are replaced as the principal figures of history by the poor and defeated, history turns out to consist largely of a series of injustices. As historical memory is gradually democratized and globalized, we have to get used to being seen not just as pioneers and benefactors, but also as oppressors and perpetrators of outrages, sometimes of continent-wide crimes.

The new historical perspective has set off a growing avalanche of claims for damages all over the world. The victims of history's crimes have been given the courage to make demands.

Not even the victims of the Holocaust had the right to damages, at the start. Former Gestapo and SS men, by contrast, received full pensions. Old Nazis stood laughing at their windows, looking down at the former owners of what had once been Jewish-owned houses. The Jews' demand for $12 billion compensation for lost property was ignored by the Allies, apart from a few million from frozen German assets abroad.

It was therefore ground-breaking when West Germany in 1951 declared itself willing to pay financial compensation to the Jewish people, and to individual Jewish victims of Nazi crimes.

The sufferings of the Jews were still not well known, as they are today through research, diaries, documents and feature films. The Jews were seen as one group among many stricken by the war. Why did they particularly deserve compensation?

East Germany did not admit any liability whatsoever for the crimes of the Third Reich. The West Germans too, both individually and collectively, were reluctant to admit guilt and responsibility.

The Ground

Is there any such thing as collective guilt or debt? Can collective debt be inherited?

It's self-evident that specific collectives, such as companies or states, can have *economic* debts. Debts of that nature carry responsibility for repayment.

But can a collective, such as a company or a people, also have a moral debt? What responsibilities does it carry, if so? Must they admit having committed an injustice? Must they say sorry? Perhaps even give back what's been taken? And if something can't be given back, like life or good health – must there be economic compensation instead? Can even moral debt imply responsibility for repayment?

Such questions are answered differently in different countries. I read in my newspaper that an American diagnosed with a brain tumour is suing a mobile-phone company for several billion dollars. Seven families who lost relatives in the 11 September attacks are demanding $100 billion in compensation from Bin Laden. Enormous damage claims are the norm in the USA.

Another day, the newspaper informs me that the asbestos workers in Lomma have had to make do with a pathetic few thousand *kronor* in compensation for their lungs. And yet it was the greatest workplace health and safety scandal in Swedish history. When the asbestos cement sheeting factory in Lomma closed in 1977, 500 workers had been affected, 150 had become invalids and 51 had died of asbestosis. Since that time, asbestos has continued claiming new victims.

Thus history lives on in the bodies of living people. When the dead body is opened up, you find history in the form of glittering silver fibres – the last remains of the air people inhaled in factories and workers' accommodation in the 1950s and 60s.

And when the votes are counted at the boardroom meetings of today's companies, the same history is there – the profits from that time still entitle their owners to power and dividends. Just as the asbestos workers' children have inherited the fibres, so other children have inherited the blocks of shares. Shouldn't they also have inherited the responsibility for the working conditions that once generated those profits?

And that applies not just to company shareholders but to all of us who have reaped the benefit of unacceptable conditions in the past. I can hear the voice of the Norwegian great-grandmother in my head. She was right. I'd had my share of the booty. So I had to take my share of the responsibility, too.

111

The Australian Aborigines' demands for redress and compensation are part of a global movement that sometimes succeeds, sometimes fails.

Of the two hundred thousand women who were forcibly recruited to Japanese military brothels during the Second World War, only a couple of thousand are left today. Public opinion in Japan views them as prostitutes. They have therefore received only half-hearted apologies and risibly meagre compensation payments.[168]

By contrast, many of the Americans of Japanese origin whom the USA interned without any justification during the same war are today influential members of society. On the basis of the precedent set by the damages Germany is paying to Israel, they were granted full redress and compensation in 1988.

The prestige enjoyed by a particular ethnic group seems to be the major factor in deciding the level of damage payments they achieve. It's a sign of the lack of respect of society at large that the Aborigines in Australia and the Sami in Sweden so often fail in their attempts to demand back the land taken from them. And it's certainly no coincidence that the very Aboriginal settlements that have won international acclaim for their art are also among those who have pursued the most successful campaign to regain control of their lands.

In the USA, a series of Native American nations has demanded that the agreements broken by the American government in the nineteenth century be reinstated. One particularly dramatic story is that of Black Hills, which is holy ground for the Sioux Indians. The US government considered the land worthless, and so let the Indians keep it. Six years later, gold was found and the land was confiscated. The Sioux have been insisting on their rights of ownership for more than a hundred years. In 1980 the US Supreme Court offered them the largest sum in damages in Native American history, $122 million. But they refused the money and are continuing to demand their land back.[169]

In other cases demands for compensation are aimed primarily at financial redress. The Herero people of Namibia are demanding apologies and compensation for the German genocide of 1904. African-Americans are demanding compensation for slavery and discrimination. In 1995, the 60 million black people in Brazil demanded $6,000 billion in compensation for slavery. In Africa, the countries from which the slaves were taken are formulating similar claims.

These are just a few examples among many of a general tendency to translate moral demands into financial ones. They are often put as counter-demands to the financial debt currently enslaving the Third World.

Many see these demands as moral blackmail and the globalization of a grotesque American compensation culture that keeps the lawyers and insurance companies rich and ultimately results in increased costs to consumers. Others see them as a practicable route to reconciliation with the past.

Can financial compensation provide release from guilt for historical crimes? Can punitively high financial dues paid to victims also prevent new victims emerging? Can they in fact lead to a new, global redistribution policy?

One advantage of this method is that it doesn't seek to achieve a single, definitive solution to all these problems, but is a way of negotiating through the problems one at a time. The more governments that acknowledge their responsibilities and compensate the victims, the easier one hopes it will become for other governments to do the same.

Is negotiation over historic debt a generally applicable method for conflict resolution? That's a question posed by historian Elazar Barkan. Can it even generate a new relationship between the powerful and the powerless? Between the rich and the poor? Can the admission of historic debt or guilt foster new cooperation between the perpetrator and the victim, to throw off the curse of the past?

Hitherto it has at least proved possible to find a few individual, temporary solutions to questions of debt and compensation in a deeply unjust world.[170]

'It's no use crying over spilt milk,' people say when someone's bemoaning losses in the past. 'Let the dead bury their dead.' Getting indignant about crimes of the past is a waste of energy. Paying compensation is 'throwing good money after bad'. Countless sayings exhort us just to forget and move on, in the knowledge that once something has happened it is beyond recall. 'What's done is done. You can't turn back the clock.'

Countering the wisdom of the proverbs is the conviction that even the past can be changed. When the misdeeds of the past are brought to light, when the perpetrators and their heirs confess and ask forgiveness, when we do penance and mend our ways and pay the price – then the crime committed has a new setting and a new significance. No longer the inescapable extinction of a people, but its ability to survive and ultimately to have the justice of its claim acknowledged.

Chronology

The events of the book organized chronologically, with the chapter in which an event is mentioned given in brackets.

600 million years before modern chronology The sandstone in Uluru begins to be formed from coarse gravel of gneiss and granite coming from the south (16).

100 million years before modern chronology Australia breaks free from Antarctica (77).

30 million years before modern chronology The silica in the groundwater accumulates in the porous sandstone and crystallizes into opals (12).

20 million years before modern chronology Australia is flooded by the sea and large areas of the south coast are covered by the world's largest limestone plateau, covering a quarter of a million square kilometres (77).

70,000 to 40,000 years befor modern chronology The Aborigines arrive in Australia.

13,000 years before modern chronology The last forest disappears from the limestone plateau, leaving the most recently formed desert, Nullarbor (77).

1770 James Cook claims eastern Australia for Great Britain.

1788 The British invasion of Australia begins. Eastern Australia becomes a penal colony.

1827 Captain James Stirling finds paradise in the Murray River valley in Western Australia (73).

1829 The first British settlers reach the Murray River (73).

1834 The Pinjarra massacre (73).

1837 A British parliamentary committee reports that the indigenous peoples of the empire are *en route* to extinction (6).

1839 John Eyre finds paradise in Moorundie (5). George Grey arrives at the islands of Bernier and Dorré, where no tree or blade of grass grows (58).

1841 Massacre of the Aboriginal population in Moorundie. Eyre becomes District Chief (5).

1862 McDouall Stuart is successful, at the third attempt, in crossing Australia from south to north. He is elevated to the peerage – and dies an alcoholic in obscurity in London four years later (8).

1871 In *The Descent of Man*, Charles Darwin presents the extermination of native peoples as a natural part of the process of evolution (20).

1877 In *Ancient Society*, Henry Morgan concludes from the Aborigines' forms of address that human beings originally lived in group marriages (34).

1884 Friedrich Engels develops Morgan's idea further: the transition from animal to human being occurred when the males relinquished their claims to sexual monopoly and began sharing females with one another (34).

1887 Baldwin Spencer becomes a professor in Melbourne, Émile Durkheim a university teacher in Bordeaux and Sigmund Freud a doctor in Vienna (26).

1888 German ethnologist Richard Andree likens Australian rock art to graffiti in public toilets (90).

1890 Catherine Martin describes the contrasts between white and black child-rearing in *An Australian Girl* (36).

1891 Frank Gillen, Justice of the Peace, intervenes in a case of routine police murder of Aborigines. The officer responsible, William Willshire, is acquitted but transferred out of the area (19).

1895 Ernest Favenc publishes *The Secret of the Australian Desert* (17,18).

1896 The report of the Horn expedition sentences the Aborigines to extinction (21). The Arrernte people respond with one of the most successful publicity campaigns in history. Spencer and Gillen are invited for seven weeks of ceremonies in the back yard of the telegraph station at Alice Springs (22).

1899 Spencer and Gillen's *The Native Tribes of Central Australia* creates a scientific sensation in Europe (22). Later in the year, Freud makes his name with *Die Traumdeutung* (*The Interpretation of Dreams*) (26). Edward Nelson's standard work *The Eskimo* is published (106).

1900 'If the workforce of a colony cannot be disciplined into producing the profits rightly expected by the mother country,' writes Henry C. Morris in his *History of Colonization*, 'the natives must then be exterminated or reduced to such numbers as to be readily controlled.' Many scholars defend or advocate what we today term genocide. (20).

1901 Australia ceases to be a British colony and becomes a self-governing federal state under the British Crown. One of the first laws the federation passes is the Immigration Restriction Act (10).

1902 Petr Kropotkin publishes *Mutual Aid*, which argues that natural selection leads not to conflict and competition but to a search for ways of avoiding conflict. Animals become humans through cooperation (25).

1903 In Jeannie Gunn's *The Little Black Princess of the Never-Never*, a white housewife tells the story of her black maid in a benevolently condescending tone. The first full-length portrait of a young Aboriginal woman in Australian literature (31).

1904 In *The Northern Tribes of Central Australia*, Spencer and Gillen dismiss the Aborigines' art as incomprehensible decoration (90).

1907 A young doctor, Paul Meunier, publishes under the name of Marcel Réja a programme for Cubism, which Picasso and Braque begin putting into practice in the autumn of the same year (96).

1908 On Bernier and Dorré, two hospitals are opened for the forcible treatment of Aborigines alleged to have sexually transmitted diseases (58).

1911 In the Northern Territory, the Aboriginals' Ordinance gives a protector appointed by the whites authority to take any Aborigine or 'half-blood' into custody at any time. The ordinance remains in force until 1957 (33). Eric Mjöberg, leader of a Swedish expedition to Australia, robs Aboriginal graves and takes the skeletons home with him (48, 49). Radcliffe-Brown studies the social organization of the Aborigines by questioning patients on Bernier and Dorré (59).

1912 In *Les Formes élémentaires de la vie réligieuse* (*The Elementary Forms of Religious Life*) Émile Durkheim reinterprets Spencer and Gillen's data in the light of his own view of society. The experience of society is the real-life basis of all religions (26).

1912–13 In *Totem und Tabu* (*Totem and Taboo*), Sigmund Freud reinterprets Spencer and Gillen's data in the light of his patients' neuroses. Patricide is the creative act that leads to the genesis of civilization (27).

1912–17 A transcontinental railway is built, linking Adelaide and Perth. The Aborigines' ceremonial site at Ooldea becomes a water reservoir for the railway (79).

1913 Borislaw Malinowski's *The Family Among the Australian Aborigines* re-evaluates the reliability of the sources of many statements about Aboriginal families and finds one fact incontrovertible: they are deeply attached to their children

(35). Baldwin Spencer establishes Kahlin Compound in Darwin as an internment camp for children taken from black mothers (41). Radcliffe-Brown begins publishing the results of his genealogical studies of the patients committed for treatment at Bernier and Dorré (60, 61).

1914 In *Gudstrons uppkomst* (*The Origin of Faith in God*), Nathan Söderblom retells the Luritja people's stories of the initial helplessness of mankind (14). A new doctor discovers that most of the patients forcibly detained on Bernier and Dorré do not have sexually transmitted diseases. Incorrect diagnosis, wrong treatment, unnecessary internment (58).

1915 A black boy finds the first opal at Coober Pedy (12).

1918 The hospital on Bernier and Dorré is closed down. All that remains on the 'Islands of the Dead' are the graves of the patients who died during treatment (58). The buildings are pulled down and taken to Moore River Native Settlement, a new reform school for children taken from their black mothers (69).

1919 Daisy Bates pitches her tent in Ooldea (79).

1921 'Unnecessary' toys are removed from Moore River Settlement and the timetable is restricted purely to physical labour. The nutritional value of the food is reduced; tuberculosis becomes increasingly common (69).

1922 While boring for more water, the railway engineers split the rock beneath the water reservoir in Ooldea (79).

1923 Catherine Martin's book *The Incredible Journey* tells of two black women's search for an abducted child (38).

1925 Margaret Preston 'discovers' the Aborigines' art, seeing it as an open treasure chest from which white artists can help themselves (91).

1927 A gang of police officers and settlers enter the Forrest River Aboriginal reservation in Kimberley and kill all the Aborigines they find. Pastor Gribble reports the mass murder and an investigation finds at least eleven of the

Aborigines had been shot while in chains. No white people are prepared to testify against the perpetrators, who boast openly of their deed. The officers return to duty; Pastor Gribble is sent elsewhere (64).

1928 Severe drought leads to water disputes. The Aborigines attempt to stop white people letting their cattle drink and pollute the water they need for survival. A white dingo hunter called Brooks is murdered. The police respond by killing Aborigines indiscriminately: the Coniston massacre (64).

1930 Mary Bennett's *The Australian Aboriginal as a Human Being* is published (64).

1932 Theo Strehlow returns to the Hermannsburg of his childhood to study the phonetics of the Arrernte language He spends fifteen years in the wilderness, collecting songs and seeing himself as the Homer of the Arrernte people (86, 87).

1933 Mary Bennett attacks official policy on native peoples, particularly the situation at Moore River. An inquiry uncovers extremely bad conditions but makes only vague recommendations (70). The United Aborigines Mission opens a mission station on the ritual site at Ooldea (80).

1935 Xavier Herbert arrives in Darwin as acting head of Kahlin Compound (41). The Museum of Modern Art in New York exhibits African art (96).

1936 Daisy Bates leaves Ooldea (79). Camel keeper Albert Namatjira learns to paint in watercolour (92).

1937 The Native Administration Act gives the Chief Protector legal instruments with which to 'breed out' the Aborigines, the 'final solution' to the race problem in Western Australia (70).

1938 Australia's first modern novel, Xavier Herbert's *Capricornia*, is a furious attack on white racism and an impassioned defence of abandoned children (39–42). The Aborigines mark the 150th anniversary of the white invasion with a Day of Mourning (70). Daisy Bates's *The Passing of the Aborigines* attempts to reconcile faith in the benevolence of the empire with a conviction that the Aborigines are doomed to extinction (79).

1939 Kahlin Compound is closed down (41).

1940 The Museum of Modern Art in New York exhibits Mexican art (96).

1941 Catherine and Ronald Berndt carry out their first fieldwork in Ooldea (80). The Museum of Modern Art in New York exhibits Native American art (96).

1945 Little Millicent is born in a sand dune behind the hospital in Geraldton (65). Noel White takes up a teaching post at Carrolup Native Settlement, 'a dumping ground for human refuse', and starts to stimulate the children through games, singing and drawing (71).

1946 The Museum of Modern Art in New York exhibits South Pacific art (96).

1947 In Woomera, launch pads are constructed for a missile-firing range 2,400 kilometres in length, mainly on land formerly allocated to the Aborigines 'in perpetuity' (9).

1948 The Nationality and Citizenship Act ostensibly gives Australian citizenship to all Australian Aborigines – but without the right to vote or any other civil rights (93).

The artist James Houston 'discovers' the art of the Inuit (106).

1949 H. E. Thonemann's *Tell the White Man: The Life Story of an Aboriginal Lubra* relates further adventures of the little black princess, narrated in the first autobiography of an Aboriginal woman (32). The police take four-year-old Millicent from her mother and six siblings and place her in a children's home (65). In *Les structures élémentaires de la parenté* (*Elementary Structures of Kinship*), Claude Lévi-Strauss shows that Aboriginal culture finds its fullest expression in its family relationships (65).

1950   Drawings from Carrolup Native Settlement win praise when exhibited in London (71).

1951   The Moore River institution is taken over by the Methodist Church (70). West Germany begins paying compensation to the Jewish people, and to individual Jewish victims of Nazi crimes (109).

1952   The mission station at Ooldea closes (80).

1953   On 15 October, a ten-kiloton atomic bomb is set off at Emu, just north of Ooldea (81). The 1953 Welfare Ordinance (NT) substitutes the racially neutral word 'ward' for 'Aborigine'. More than 99 per cent of the Aboriginal population are declared 'wards' of the state (93). The Museum of Modern Art in New York mounts a further exhibition of African art (96).

1956   Nancy D. Munn arrives at Yuendumu and begins researching the uses and meanings of the Warlpiri people's pictures (95).

1956–7   Seven British atomic bombs are exploded near Maralinga, just west of Ooldea (81).

1957   Namatjira is rewarded for his artistic achievement with Australian citizenship (93). The Museum of Primitive Art opens in New York (96).

1957–63   At Maralinga, the British defy the Nuclear Test Ban Treaty by carrying out 'minor trials', releasing at least twenty kilograms of plutonium which spread over wide areas in the form of fine dust (81).

1958   The Migration Act allows every foreigner without a visa to be interned (10). The Western Australian police defend the use of neck-irons by saying the natives want to wear them (58).

1959   Albert Namatjira is sentenced to three months' hard labour for having supplied a relative with intoxicating liquor, and interned in Papunya. Having served his sentence, he dies of a heart attack. He is buried on 9 August after two years as an Australian citizen (93).

1962 Millicent is sent as a maid to a station where she is raped by her white employer. She seeks refuge at the children's home, but is ordered back to the station, where she is tortured and raped again. She gives birth to a child which is taken from her (66).

Aboriginal people acquire the right to vote in both state and Commonwealth elections. They are however still 'wards' of the state and subject to the rulings of the Director of Welfare (93).

1964 The Social Welfare Ordinance (NT) abolishes the concept of 'ward' and replaces it with 'persons who in the opinion of the Director are socially or economically in need of assistance'. The change in terms changes little in the authorities' practice of power (93).

1965 Colin Johnson publishes his first book, *Wild Cat Falling*, Australia's first Aboriginal novel. Writing under the name Mudrooroo, Johnson soon becomes the leading novelist of Aboriginal literature (72).

1966 Inspired by the civil rights movement in the United States, the workers at Black Hill Station go on strike, first for wages, then for land (44). Aboriginal people are included in the Australian social security system. Their social benefits are, however, often not paid out to them personally, but to their employer or to the institution in which they are confined (93).

1967 In a referendum 90 per cent of Australians vote YES to changing the Constitution so as to include Aboriginal people in the national census. The referendum has great symbolic significance, but the fight for full citizenship rights goes on well into the 1980s (93).

1968 After repeated decontamination operations round Maralinga, an agreement absolves the British from any further responsibility for consequences of the atomic tests. The area is checked again. Plutonium is found to have been ploughed only a few decimetres into the ground, and exposed again by the harsh desert winds (82).

1970–1 Historian C. D. Rowley publishes *The Destruction of Aboriginal Society*, a pioneering work attempting for the first time to see Australian history from an Aboriginal point of view (107).

1971 Theo Strehlow publishes his magnum opus *The Songs of Central Australia* (86–9, 98, 103). So-called primitive art reaches the world's most exclusive museum venue: the Metropolitan Museum of Art in New York (96). Geoffrey Bardon arrives at Papunya. His interest triggers a flurry of artistic activity. The men begin translating their traditional pictorial idiom into modern acrylic paintings (99–103, 106, 107).

1972 Geoffrey Bardon leaves Papunya, convinced he has been defeated (100). A left-wing government takes office and implements new policies on Aborigines, and successors to Bardon handle the administration and marketing of Papunya art (101).

1973 Nancy D. Munn publishes her study of the pictorial world of the desert: *Walbiri Iconography* (94, 95).

1974 The camp authorities vandalize the wall paintings at Papunya (101).

1975 The strike at Wave Hill ends with the Gurundji people regaining 3,200 square kilometres of land they had lost.

1977 When the asbestos cement sheeting factory in Lomma, Sweden, closes, 500 workers are suffering ill effects, 150 have become invalids and 51 have died of asbestosis. Since that time, asbestos has claimed new victims year after year (109).

1978 Theo Strehlow dies the same day his research institute is due to open. His last words are 'Oblivion that has no end' (87).

1979 The Australian Nuclear Veterans' Association is formed; hundreds of experts and ex-soldiers start giving their account of events. The British resume the decontamination process but only retrieve half a kilogram of plutonium. At least 19kg remain in the desert sand (82).

Chronology

1980 The South Australian Museum hangs Clifford Possum's *Man's Love Story* with other works by contemporary artists. The painting immediately dominates the huge gallery (101). The US Supreme Court offers the Sioux the highest compensation award in American Indian history, $122 million. They refuse the money and continue demanding to be given back the Black Hills (110).

1981–3 The art movement spreads to Papunya's offshoots at Kintore and Kiwirkurra (105).

1983 Sixteen-year-old John Pat is taken into custody on 28 September after a clash between Aborigines and the police in Roebourne. He dies in his cell the same night. Five officers are accused of murder, but acquitted (55).

1984 A royal commission demands that the British authorities make Maralinga safe for permanent resettlement by the indigenous population, who by the Maralinga Land Rights Act regain the land requisitioned from them in the 1950s (82). A group of ritually active women in Yuendumu follow Papunya's example and begin to paint (104).

1985 Uluru is restored to its original owners, the Anangu people – on condition that the area remains accessible to tourists. Uluru becomes the central national symbol in the marketing of Australia as a tourist destination (16). The art movement spreads to Balgo (105).

1986–7 Aborigines at Lajamanu, Utopia and a number of other desert settlements begin painting (105).

1987 The Stuart Highway is tarmacked all the way from Adelaide to Darwin (8). The 'songlines' found by Nancy D. Munn among the Warlpiri people become world-famous through Bruce Chatwin's book *The Songlines* (94).

1988 Five years after John Pat's death, an investigation is launched; its final report, 'Black Deaths in Custody', alerts the whole nation to racist police violence (55). Desert art makes its international breakthrough thanks to the

Dreamings exhibition in New York, Chicago and Los Angeles (101). Americans of Japanese descent, forcibly interned during the Second World War, are given redress and financial compensation (110).

1990   Four hundred delegates from indigenous peoples in 120 countries assemble for the first Continental Indigenous International Convention in Quito (108).

1991   Australia begins a decade-long process of reconciliation between white and black with a Year of the Indigenous Peoples. Prime Minister Keating says: 'It was we who did the dispossessing. We committed the murders' (108).

1992   In the Mabo Decision, the Australian Supreme Court outlaws the concept of '*terra nullius*', thus revising the whole historic and legal basis of Australia as a nation (108).

1995   Brazil's six million black people demand $6,000 billion in compensation for slavery (110).

1996   Millicent is reunited with her daughter Tony, taken from her thirty-three years earlier (66). Doris Pilkington's documentary novel *Follow the Rabbit-Proof Fence* describes the fate of children running away from the Moore River Settlement (70). A Conservative government comes to power and announces: 'Australians of this generation should not be required to accept guilt and blame for past actions and policies' (108).

1999   Woomera (10) and Curtin (50) become internment camps for asylum seekers.

2001   A painting by Rover Thomas is sold for over three-quarters of a million dollars (105). Fences and warning signs still encircle Maralinga. It will take 280,000 years for half the radiation in the plutonium dust to subside (82).

2002   Hunger-striking prisoners at Woomera sew up their mouths (10). At Curtin, they burn down the camp (50). The Moore River Settlement is made internationally known by the film *Rabbit-Proof Fence* (70).

Thirty years of professional scholarship on Aboriginal

history come under attack by journalist historians, who try to re-establish Australians' pride in their history by denying genocide, mass killings and forced dispossession (109).

2003 Geoffrey Bardon dies in Taree after a long period of illness (102).

Notes

To Moorundie

1. Salomon; Lindley; *Dictionnaire*; Bedjaoui; Anaya.
2. Tindale, p. 214; Mulvaney, Ch. 12.
3. Eyre, pp.147 ff.
4. Dutton, pp. 66, 71, 157–65.
5. Mulvaney, Ch. 12.
6. Report of the Parliamentary Select Committee on Aboriginal Tribes, 1837.
7. Eyre, Ch. 1.

The Secret of the Desert

8. Mudie.
9. Morton, Chs. 4–6; Southall; Beadell; Chambers.
10. Immigration Museum, Adelaide; Jupp, Ch. 5.
11. McMaster, Preface, Chs. 3, 4, 6; Immigration Museum, Adelaide.
12. McMaster, p. 95.
13. White, Ch. 4.
14. White, Chs. 18, 23.
15. Söderblom, Ch. 4.
16. White, Ch. 7.
17. Favenc, Ch. 4.
18. Favenc, Ch. 5.
19. Favenc, Ch. 7.
20. Favenc, Ch. 8; see also Phillips, Ch. 4, Haynes, Ch 5.
21. Favenc, Ch. 25.

22. Mulvaney, Ch. 18.
23. Dewar, Ch. 2.
24. Mulvaney, Ch. 18.
25. Darwin, Ch. 6; Lindqvist, *Exterminate*; Lindqvist, *The Skull Measurer's Mistake*, Chs. 10, 12, 18.
26. George Chatterton Hill, Ch. 5.
27. Morris, p. 20 f.
28. Pitt-Rivers, Ch. 3.
29. *Report on the Work of the Horn Scientific Expedition to Central Australia*, Vol. 4, p. iv.
30. Spencer and Gillen called them 'Arunta', and various other forms of the name occur in the literature. I use throughout the name that the Aborigine peoples themselves use today.
31. Stocking; Mulvaney and Calaby, Ch. 9.
32. Malinowski, quoted in Gill, Ch. 2.
33. *New Territory News*, 24 March 2003.
34. Kropotkin; Woodcock; Hiatt, Ch. 5.
35. Hiatt, Ch. 6.
36. Gay, Ch. 1.
37. Lukes; Kuper, Ch. 6.
38. Freud, *Totem und Tabu*, Part IV, Ch. 5.
39. Freud, *Totem und Tabu*, Part IV, Ch. 7.
40. Gay, Ch. 7.
41. Lukes, Ch. 23.

To Kahlin Compound

42. Wright, Ch. 6.
43. Wright, Ch. 3.
44. Wright, Ch. 3
45. Wright, Ch. 5
46. Wright, Ch. 4.
47. Gunn, Ch. 3.
48. Gunn, Ch. 11.
49. Gunn, Ch. 9.
50. Dewar, Ch. 2.
51. Thonemann, Ch. 1.

52. Thonemann, Ch. 10.
53. Thonemann, p. 66.
54. *Bringing them Home*, Ch. 7.
55. *Bringing them Home*, Ch. 9.
56. Hiatt, Ch.3.
57. Engels, pp. 39–55; Kuper, Ch. 3; Hiatt, Ch. 4.
58. Kuper, Ch. 6.
59. Malinowski, Ch. 1; cf. Engels, p. 49: 'Not the individuals but the whole group are married to each other, class with class.'
60. Malinowski, Introduction.
61. Martin, *An Australian Girl*, Ch. 16.
62. Pierce, Introduction.
63. Martin, *The Incredible Journey*, Ch. 8.
64. Martin, *The Incredible Journey*, Ch. 26
65. Quoted in Dewar, Ch.4; Haynes, Ch. 10.
66. Herbert, Ch. 3.
67. Herbert, Ch. 4.
68. Herbert, Ch. 7.
69. Herbert, Ch. 10.
70. Herbert, Ch. 11.
71. Herbert, Ch. 14.
72. McGregor, Ch. 4.
73. De Groen, Ch. 6.
74. De Groen, Ch. 10.
75. Herbert, Ch. 32.

The Dead Do Not Die

76. Rowley, *The Remote Aborigines*, Ch. 16; Attwood and Markus, sections 124–8.
77. Mjöberg, *Bland vilda djur och folk i Australien*, Ch. 18. Translations into English from the original Swedish by Sarah Death.
78. Mjöberg, *Bland vilda*, Ch. 21.
79. Mjöberg, *Bland vilda*, Ch. 22.
80. Mjöberg, *Bland vilda*, Ch. 25.
81. Tyler, Ch. 1.
82. Ernestine Hill, *The Great Australian Loneliness*, Ch. 4.
83. Edwards, Ch. 5.

84. *Bringing them Home*, Ch. 1, confidential evidence 821.
85. Attwood and Markus, section 165.
86. Eyre, entries for 24 February to 1 March 1839.
87. Jebb; Mulvaney, Ch. 26.
88. Watson, Ch. 15.
89. Radcliffe-Brown, 'Three Tribes of Western Australia'.
90. Bates, Ch. 9; Salter, Ch. 17.

To Pinjarra

91. Critique of Radcliffe-Brown in Shapiro.
92. Bennett, *Christison of Lammermoor*, Ch. 7.
93. Bennett, *The Australian Aboriginal as a Human Being*, Ch. 3; Rowley, Ch. 11.
94. Elder, Chs. 14, 15.
95. Bennett, *The Australian Aboriginal*, Ch. 4.
96. *Australian Dictionary of Biography*, Ch. 7.
97. *Bringing them Home*, Ch. 7, confidential submission 640.
98. Lévi-Strauss, Ch. 11.
99. *Bringing them Home*, Ch. 7.
100. Christopher Johnson, Ch. 2.
101. Leach, Ch. 6.
102. Quoted in Clarke, Ch. 2.
103. Quoted in Clarke, Ch. 4
104. Lévi-Strauss, Ch. 23.
105. Quoted in Clarke, Ch. 4.
106. Clarke, Ch. 5.
107. Haebich, Ch. 5.
108. Haebich, Ch. 5.
109. Haebich, Ch. 6.
110. Haebich, Ch. 10.
111. Haebich, Ch. 6.
112. Durack, Ch. 4.
113. Durack, Chs. 5–7.
114. Durack, Chs. 10, 14.
115. Colin Johnson, Preface.
116. Colin Johnson, Ch. 4.
117. Colin Johnson, Ch. 10.

118. Rowley, *The Destruction of Aboriginal Society*, Ch. 4; Mulvaney, Ch. 24.

The Smell of White Man

119. Shephard, Introduction.
120. White, Chs. 5, 7.
121. Shephard, Chs. 6 , 8.
122. Bates; Ernestine Hill, *The Great Australian Loneliness*.
123. Ernestine Hill, *Kabbarli*, Ch. 1.
124. Salter, Ch. 18.
125. Blackburn, Ch. 22.
126. Blackburn, Ch. 15.
127. Ernestine Hill, *Kabbarli*, Ch. 10.
128. Berndt, Ch. 4.
129. Shephard, Ch. 5; Beadell, Ch. 16; Blakeway, Ch. 6.
130. Shephard, Ch. 9.

The Ground

131. Barry Hill.
132. Strehlow, 'Geography and the Totemic Landscape in Central Australia'.
133. Barry Hill, pp. 166 ff., 441 ff.
134. Strehlow, *Songs of Cental Australia*.
135. Barry Hill, p. 752.
136. Molnar and Meadows.
137. Grey, Vol. 1, p. 263.
138. Andree, p. 64.
139. Eylmann, Chs. 5, 23.
140. Spencer and Gillen, *The Native Tribes of Central Australia*, Ch. 19.
141. Spencer and Gillen, *The Northern Tribes of Central Australia*, Ch. 25.
142. Haynes, Ch. 5.
143. Foy.
144. Kühn, Ch.7.
145. Haynes, Ch. 15
146. Barrett and Croll; Mountford, 1944; Battarbee.

Notes

147. Chesterman and Galligan.
148. Batty, Ch. 13.
149. Mountford, 1937.
150. Munn, Ch. 5.
151. Munn, Ch. 4.
152. Errington.
153. Bardon, *Aboriginal Art of the Western Desert*; Ryan and Bardon, *Mythscapes*; Bardon, *Papunya Tule*; Amadin and Kimber; Caruana, *Windows on the Dreaming*; Vivien Johnson, *Aboriginal Artists of the Western Desert*; Corbally Stourton; Morphy; *Papunya Tula.*
154. Bardon, *Papunya Tula*, p. 45.
155. Vivien Johnson, *Aboriginal Artists*, Ch. 4; Radford.
156. Sutton, *Dreaming*; Myers, *Painting Culture.*
157. Warlukurlangi Artists, Ryan and Bardon, *Mythscapes*; Vivien Johnson, *Aboriginal Arists*, Ch. 2; Dussart, *A Body Painting in Translation*; Dussart, *The Politics of Ritual in an Aboriginal Settlement*, Ch. 3.
158. Dussart, *The Politics of Ritual*, Ch. 3.
159. Geoff Maslen, 'Aboriginal Art Set to Top $15 million', *The Age*, 7 July 2004.
160. Himmelheber; Graburn; Ray; Crandall.
161. Reynolds.
162. Rowley, *The Destruction of Aboriginal Society*, Ch. 2.
163. Rowley, *The Destruction of Aboriginal Society*, Ch. 3.
164. Brandström; Lundmark, *Så länge vi. har marker*; Lundmark, 'Lappen är ombytlig, ostadig och obekväm'.
165. Barkan, Ch. 10.
166. This chapter has been added to the English edition. Records of the Windschuttle debate in Manne and Dawson. Attwood & Foster, Macintyre and Attwood analyze the revisionist attack from historical and ethical perspectives. Meanwhile the scholarly discussion continues, for example in Moses.
167. Quoted in Torpey.
168. Hicks.
169. Barkan, Ch. 8; Lazarus, Chs 16, 17.
170. Barkan, particularly the Introduction and Conclusion.

Bibliography

For practical guidance I have relied on the Lonely Planet guides. My most important historical reference tool has been D. J. Mulvaney's *Encounters in Place*. I have studied issues of historical guilt principally in Elazar Barkan's *The Guilt of Nations*. My teacher on the subject of Australian nature study has been Mary E. White, in particular her *After the Greening*. My spiritual guide to the desert has been, and will remain, *Seeking the Centre* by Roslynn D. Haynes.

Amadio, Nadine, and Kimber, Richard, *Wildbird Dreaming: Aboriginal Art from the Central Deserts of Australia*, Melbourne, 1988.

Anaya, James, *Indigenous Peoples in International Law*, Oxford, 1996.

Andree, Richard, *Ethnographische Parallelen und Vergleiche, Neue Folge*, Stuttgart, 1888.

Attwood, Bain, *Telling the Truth about Aboriginal History*, Sydney, 2005.

Attwood, Bain and Foster, S. G. *Frontier Conflict: The Australian Experience*, Canberra, 2003.

Attwood, Bain, and Markus, Andrew, *The Struggle for Aboriginal Rights: A Documentary History*, Melbourne, 1999.

Australian Dictionary of Biography, Vol. 7, Melbourne, 1979.

Bardon, Geoff, *Aboriginal Art of the Western Desert*, Adelaide, 1979.

Bardon, Geoffrey, *Papunya Tula: Art of the Western Desert*, New York, 1991.

Barrett, Charles, and Croll, Robert Henderson, *Art of the Australian Aboriginal*, Melbourne, 1943.

Barkan, Elazar, *The Guilt of Nations: Restitution and Negotiating Historical Injustices*, New York, 2000.

Bibliography

Basedow, Herbert, *The Australian Aboriginal*, Adelaide, 1925.

Bates, Daisy, *The Passing of the Aborigines: A Lifetime Spent Among the Natives of Australia*, London, 1938.

Battarbee, Rex, *Modern Australian Aboriginal Art*, Sydney, 1951.

Batty, Joyce D. *Namatjira: Wanderer Between Two Worlds*, Melbourne, 1963.

Beadell, Len, *Still in the Bush*, (1965), Sydney, 1999.

—— *Blast the Bush*, Sydney, (1967), 1999.

Bedjaoui, Mohammed, *Terra nullius, 'droits' historiques et autodétermination: Exposés oraux devant la Cour internationale de Justice*, La Haye, 1975.

Bennett, Mary Montgomerie, *The Australian Aboriginal as a Human Being*, London, 1930.

—— *Christison of Lammermoor*, London, 1927.

Berndt, Catherine and Ronald, *From Black to White in South Australia*, Melbourne, 1951.

Blackburn, Julia, *Daisy Bates in the Desert: A Woman's Life Among the Aborigines*, London, 1994.

Blakeway, Denys and Lloyd-Roberts, Sue, *Fields of Thunder: Testing Britain's Bomb*, London, 1985.

Bolinder, Gustaf, *Naturfolkens konst*, Stockholm, 1927.

Boulter, Michael, *The Art of Utopia: A New Direction in Contemporary Aboriginal Art*, East Roseville, NSW, 1991.

Bringing Them Home: Report of the National Inquiry into the Separation of Aboriginal and Torres Strait Islander Children from Their Families, Canberra, 1997.

Brändström, Kjell-Arne, *Bilden av det samiska: Samerna och det samiska i skönlitteratur, forskning och debatt*, Umeå, 2000.

Cambridge Companion to Australian Literature, Cambridge, 2000.

Caruana, Wally, *Aboriginal Art*, London, 1993.

—— ed., *Windows on the Dreaming: Aboriginal Paintings in the Australian National Gallery*, Canberra, 1989.

Chambers, Edward W., *Woomera: Its Human Face*, Adelaide, 2000.

Chambers, John H., *Historisk guide till Australien*, Falun, 1999.

Chatwin, Bruce, *The Songlines*, (1987), London, 1998.

Chesterman, John and Galligan, Brian, *Citizens Without Rights: Aborigines and Australian Citizenship*, Cambridge, 1997.

Clancy, Laurie, *Xavier Herbert*, Boston, 1981.

Clarke, Simon, *The Foundations of Structuralism: A Critique of Lévi-Strauss and the Structuralist Movement*, Brighton. 1981.

Connor, Michael, *The Invention of Terra Nullius*, Sydney, 2005.

Corbally Stourton, Patrick and Nigel, *Songlines and Dreamings: Contemporary Australian Aboriginal Painting: The First Quarter-Century of Papunya Tula*, London, 1996.

Crandall, Richard C., *Inuit Art: A History*, Jefferson, NC, 2000.

Darwin, Charles, *The Origin of Species by Means of Natural Selection*, (1859), London, 1988.

—— *The Descent of Man*, (1871), Princeton, 1981.

Dawson, John, *Washout: On the Academic Response to the Fabrication of Aboriginal History*, Sydney, 2004.

Dictionnaire de la terminologie du droit international, Paris, 1960.

De Groen, Frances, *Xavier Herbert: A Biography*, Brisbane, 1998.

Dewar, Mickey, *In Search of the Never-Never: Looking for Australia in Northern Territory Writing*, Darwin, 1997.

Dixon, Robert, *Writing the Colonial Adventure: Race, Gender and Nation in Anglo-Australian Popular Fiction 1875–1914*, Cambridge, 1995.

Dreamings of the Desert: Aboriginal Dot Paintings of the Western Desert, Art Gallery of South Australia, Adelaide, 1996.

Durack Miller, Mary, *Child Artists of the Australian Bush*, London, 1952.

Durkheim, Émile, *Les Formes élémentaires de la vie religieuse*, (1912), Paris, 1998.

—— *Selected Writings*, Cambridge, 1972.

Dussart, Françoise, 'A Body Painting in Translation'. In Banks, Marcus: *Rethinking Visual Anthropology*, New Haven, CT, 1997.

—— *La Peinture des Aborigènes d'Australie*, Paris, 1993.

—— *The Politics of Ritual in an Aboriginal Settlement: Kinship, Gender and the Currency of Knowledge*, Washington DC, 2000.

Dutton, Geoffrey *The Hero as Murderer: The Life of Edward John Eyre*, London, 1967.

Edwards, Hugh, *Port of Pearls*, Perth, 1984.

Elder, Bruce, *Blood on the Wattle, Massacres and Maltreatment of Aboriginal Australians Since 1788*, Sydney, 1998.

Engels, Friedrich, *Der Ursprung der Familie, des Privateigentums und des Staats*, (1884), Berlin 1984.

Bibliography

Errington, Shelly, *The Death of Authentic Primitive Art*, Berkeley, CA, 1998.

Eylmann, Erhard, *Die Eingeborenen der Kolonie Südaustralien*, Berlin, 1908.

Eyre, Edward John, *Journals of Expeditions of Discovery into Central Australia*, Vol. 2, London, 1845.

Favenc, Ernest, *The Secrets of the Australian Desert*, (1896), *Ödemarkens hemlighet, Äventyr under en upptäcktsfärd i Australien*, Stockholm 1918.

Foy, Willy, *Führer durch das Rautenstrauch-Joest Museum der Stadt Coln*, Köln, 1906.

Freud, Sigmund, *Totem und Tabu. Einige Übereinstimmungen im Seelenleben der Wilden und der Neurotiker*, (1912–13), Frankfurt, 1974.

—— *Die Traumdeutung*, (1899), Frankfurt, 1972.

Gay, Peter, *Freud: A Life for Our Time*, New York, 1988.

Gill, Sam D., *Storytracking: Texts, Stories and Histories in Central Australia*, New York, 1998.

Glowczewski, Barbara, *Du Rêve à la loi chez les Aborigènes: Mythes, rites et organisation sociale en Australie*, Paris, 1991.

—— *Les Rêveurs du désert: Les Warlpiri*, Paris, 1989.

Goodwin, Ken, *A History of Australian Literature*, Basingstoke, 1986.

Graburn, Nelson H. H., *Ethnic and Tourist Arts: Cultural Expressions From the Fourth World*, Berkeley, CA, 1976.

Grey, George, *Journals of Two Expeditions of Discovery in Northwest and Western Australia ... With Observations on the Moral and Physical Condition of the Aboriginal Inhabitants*, London, 1841.

Grosse, Ernst, *Die Anfänge der Kunst*, Freiburg and Leipzig, 1894.

Gunn, Mrs Aeneas (Jeannie), *The Little Black Princess of the Never-Never*, (1903), Sydney, 1962.

—— *We of the Never-Never*, (1908), Sydney, 1990.

Haebich, Anna, *For Their Own Good: Aborigines and Government in the Southwest of Western Australia 1900–1940*, Crawley, WA, 1988.

Hallgren, Claes, *Två resenärer, två bilder av Australien: Eric Mjöbergs och Yngve Laurells vetenskapliga expeditioner 1910–1913*, Uppsala, 2003.

Haynes, Roslynn, *Seeking the Centre: The Australian Desert in Literature, Art and Film*, Cambridge, 1998.

Healy, J. J., *Literature and the Aborigine in Australia 1770–1975*, New York, 1978.

Herbert, Xavier, *Capricornia*, (1938), Sydney, 1999.

Hiatt, L. R., *Arguments About Aborigines: Australia and the Evolution of Social Anthropology*, Cambridge, 1996.

Hicks, George, *The Comfort Women*, Sydney, 1995.

Hill, Barry, *Broken Song: T. G. H. Strehlow and Aboriginal Possession*, Sydney, 2002.

Hill, Ernestine, *The Great Australian Loneliness*, Melbourne, 1940.

—— *Kabbarli: A Personal Memoir of Daisy Bates*, Sydney, 1973.

Hill, George Chatterton, *Heredity and Selection*, London, 1907.

Himmelheber, Hans, *Eskimo Artists*, Fairbanks, AK, 1993.

Isaacs, Jennifer, *Spirit Country: Contemporary Australian Aboriginal Art*, San Francisco, 1999.

Jebb, Mary Anne, 'The Lock Hospitals Experiment: Europeans, Aborigines and Venereal Disease', *Studies in Western Australian History VIII*, Perth, 1984.

Johnson, Christopher, *Claude Lévi-Strauss: The Formative Years*, Cambridge, 2003.

Johnson, Colin, *Wild Cat Falling*, (1965), Sydney, 1995. *See also* Mudrooroo.

Johnson, Vivien, *Aboriginal Artists of the Western Desert: A Biographical Dictionary*, Roseville, NSW, 1994.

—— *The Art of Clifford Possum Tjapaltjarri*, East Roseville, NSW, 1994.

Jupp, James, *Immigration*, Oxford, 1991.

Kropotkin, Petr, *Mutual Aid: A Factor of Evolution*, (1902), Boston, 1955.

Kühn, Herbert, *Die Kunst der Primitiven*, München, 1923.

Kuper, Adam, *The Invention of Primitive Society: Transformations of an Illusion*, London, 1988.

Lazarus, Edward, *Black Hills, White Justice: The Sioux Nation Versus the United States 1775 to the Present*, New York, 1991.

Leach, Edmund, *Claude Lévi-Strauss*, (1970), Chicago, 1978.

Lévi-Strauss, Claude, *Les Structures élémentaires de la parenté*, Paris, 1949.

Lindley, M. F., *The Acquisition and Government of Backward Territory in International Law, Being a Treatise on the Law and Practice Relating to Colonial Expansion*, New York ,1926.

Lindqvist, Sven, '*Exterminate all the Brutes*', London, 1996.

—— *The Skull Measurer's Mistake*, New York, 1997.

—— *A History of Bombing*, London, 2001.

Bibliography

Lukes, Steven, *Emile Durkheim: His Life and Work*, London, 1973.

Lumholtz, Carl, *Among Cannibals*, London, 1890.

Lundmark, Lennart, *Så länge vi har marker: Samerna och staten under sex hundra år*, Stockholm, 1999.

—— *'Lappen är ombytlig, ostadig och obekväm': Svenska statens samepolitik i rasismens tidevarv*, Umeå, 2002.

McCulloch, Susan, *Contemporary Aboriginal Art: A Guide to the Rebirth of an Ancient Culture*, Sydney, 2001.

McGregor, Russell, *Imagined Destinies: Aboriginal Australians and the Doomed Race Theory 1880–1939*, Melbourne, 1997.

Macintyre, Stuart, *The History Wars*, Carlton, Victoria, 2004.

—— (ed), *The Historian's Conscience: Australian Historians on the Ethics of History*, Melbourne, 2004.

McMaster, Don, *Asylum Seekers: Australia's Response to Refugees*, Melbourne. 2001.

Malinowski, B., *The Family Among the Australian Aborigines: A Sociological Study*, (1913), New York, 1963.

Manne, Robert, (ed) *Whitewash: On Keith Windschuttle's Fabrication of Aboriginal History* Melbourne, 2003.

Martin, Catherine, *An Australian Girl*, (1890), Oxford, 1999.

—— *The Incredible Journey*, (1923), London, 1987.

Michaels, Eric, *Bad Aboriginal Art: Tradition, Media and Technological Horizons*, Minneapolis, 1994.

Mjöberg, Eric, *Bland vilda djur och folk i Australien*, Stockholm, 1915.

—— 'Svenska Biologiska Expeditionen till Australien 1910–11', in *Ymer*, 1912:4.

Molnar, Helen and Meadows, Michael, *Songlines to Satellites: Indigenous Communication in Australia, the South Pacific and Canada*, Sydney, 2001.

Morgan, Lewis H., *Ancient Society or Researches in the Lines of Human Progress from Savagery Through Barbarism to Civilization*, New York, 1877.

Morphy, Howard, *Aboriginal Art*, London, 1998.

Morris, Henry C., *The History of Colonization From the Earliest Times to the Present Day*, New York, 1900.

Morton, Peter, *Fire Across the Desert: Woomera and the Anglo-Australian Joint Project 1946–1980*, Canberra, 1989.

Morton, S. R., and Mulvaney, D. J., *Exploring Central Australia:*

Society, the Environment and the 1894 Horn Expedition, Chipping Norton, 1996.

Moses, Dirk (ed), *Genocide and Settler Society: Frontier Violence and Stolen Indigenous Children in Australian History*, New York, 2005.

Mountford, C. P., Aboriginal Crayon Drawings From the Warburton Ranges of Western Australia Relating to the Wanderings of Two Ancestral Beings the Wati Kutjara, *Records of the South Australian Museum*, Vol. 6: 1, 1937.

—— *The Art of Albert Namatjira*, Melbourne, 1944.

Mowaljarlai, David, and Malnic, Jutta, *YorroYorro: Everything Standing up Alive*, Broome, WA, 1993.

Mudie, Ian, *The Heroic Journey of John McDouall Stuart*, Sydney, 1968.

Mudrooroo, *The Indigenous Literature of Australia*, Melbourne, 1997. *See also* Johnson, Colin.

Mulvaney, D. J., *Encounters in Place: Outsiders and Aboriginal Australians 1606–1985*, Adelaide, 1989.

Mulvaney, D. J., and Calaby, J. H., *'So Much That Is New': Baldwin Spencer 1860–1929*, Melbourne, 1985.

Munn, Nancy D., *Walbiri Iconography: Graphic Representation and Cultural Symbolism in a Central Australian Society*, Ithaca, NY, 1973.

Myers, Fred R., *Painting Culture: The Making of an Aboriginal High Art*, Durham, 2002.

—— *Pintupi Country, Pintupi Self: Sentiment, Place and Politics Among Western Desert Aborigines*, Washington, 1986.

Nelson, Edward, *The Eskimo About Bering Strait*, Washington DC, 1899.

Oxford Companion to Australian History, Melbourne, 1998.

Oxford Literary Guide to Australia, Oxford, 1993.

Papunya Tula: Genesis and Genius, Art Gallery of New South Wales, 2000.

Phillips, Richard, *Mapping Men and Empire: A Geography of Adventure*, London, 1997.

Pierce, Peter, *The Country of Lost Children: An Australian Anxiety*, Cambridge, 1999.

Pilkington, Doris, *Follow the Rabbit-Proof Fence*, Brisbane, 1996.

Pitt-Rivers, George Henry Lane-Fox, *The Clash of Cultures and the Contact of Races: An Anthropological and Psychological Study of the*

Bibliography

Laws of Racial Adaptability With Special Reference to the Depopulation of the Pacific and the Government of Subject Races, London, 1927.

Radcliffe-Brown, A. R., 'Three Tribes of Western Australia', *Journal of the Royal Anthropological Institute*, pp. 143–94, London, 1913.

—— *Social Organization of Australian Tribes*, Vols. 1–3, Oceania, 1930–1.

Radford, Ron, Preface to *Dreamings of the Desert*, Adelaide, 1996.

Ray, Dorothy Jean, *Eskimo Art*, Vancouver, 1977.

Réja, Marcel, *L'Art chez les fous*, Paris, 1907.

—— *Les Rêves et leur interprétation*, Paris, 1910.

Report of the Parliamentary Select Committee on Aboriginal Tribes, London, 1837.

Report on the Work of the Horn Scientific Expedition to Central Australia, Vol 4, *Anthropology*, Melbourne, 1896.

Reynolds, Henry, *Why Weren't We Told?: A Personal Search for the Truth about our History*, Penguin, 1999.

Rivers, William Halse Rivers, 'The Genealogical Method of Anthropological Inquiry', *Sociological Review*, 1910.

Roberts, Tony, *Frontier Justice: A History of the Gulf Culture to 1900*, St Lucia, Queensland, 2005.

Rowley, C. D., *The Destruction of Aboriginal Society, Aboriginal Policy and Practice*, Vol. 1, Canberra, 1970.

—— *The Remote Aborigines, Aboriginal Policy and Practice*, Vol. 3, Canberra, 1971.

Ryan, Judith, *Images of Power: Aboriginal Art of the Kimberley*, Melbourne, 1993.

Ryan, Judith, and Bardon, Geoffrey, *Mythscapes: Aboriginal Art of the Desert from the National Gallery of Victoria*, Melbourne, 1989.

Salomon, C., *L'Occupation des territoires sans maître*, Paris, 1889.

Salter, Elizabeth, *Daisy Bates: 'The Great White Queen of the Never Never'*, Sydney, 1972.

Shapiro, Warren, *Social Organisation in Aboriginal Australia*, New York, 1979.

Shephard, Mark, *The Great Victoria Desert*, Chatswood, NSW, 1995.

Söderblom, Nathan, *Gudstrons uppkomst*, Stockholm, 1914.

Southall, Ivan, *Woomera*, Sydney, 1962.

Spencer, W. Baldwin, and Gillen, F. J., *The Native Tribes of Central Australia*, London, 1899.

—— *The Northern Tribes of Central Australia*, London, 1904.

—— *The Arunta: A Study of a Stone Age People*, (1927), Oosterhout, 1966.

Stocking, George W, ed., *Observers Observed: Essays on Ethnographic Fieldwork*, Madison, WI, 1983.

Stokes, J. Lort, *Discoveries in Australia*, London, 1846.

Strehlow, T., 'Geography and the Totemic Landscape in Central Australia: A Functional Study', in Berndt, Ronald M. ed, *Australian Aboriginal Anthropology*, Crawley, WA, 1970.

—— *Songs of Central Australia*, Sydney, 1971.

Sutton, Peter, *Dreamings: The Art of Aboriginal Australia*, New York, 1988.

—— 'Icons of Country: Topographic Representations in Classical Aboriginal Traditions', *History of Cartography*, Vol. 2, Chicago, 1998.

—— 'Aboriginal Maps and Plans', *History of Cartography*, Vol. 2, Chicago, 1998.

Symonds, J. L., *A History of British Atomic Tests in Australia*, Canberra, 1985.

Thonemann, H. E., *Tell the White Man: The Life Story of an Aboriginal Lubra*, Sydney, 1949.

Tindale, Norman B., *Aboriginal Tribes of Australia: Their Terrain, Environmental Controls, Distribution, Limits and Proper Names*, Berkeley, CA, 1974.

Torpey, John, ed., *Politics and the Past: On Repairing Historical Injustices*, Lanham, 2003.

Tyler, Heather, *Asylum: Voices Behind the Razor Wire*, Melbourne, 2003.

Warlukurlangu Artists, *Kuruwarri, Yuendumu Doors*, Canberra, 1992.

Watson, E. L., *But to What Purpose: The Autobiography of a Contemporary*, London, 1946.

White, Mary E., *After the Greening: The Browning of Australia*, East Roseville, NSW, 1998.

Windschuttle, Keith, *The Fabrication of Aboriginal History*, Sydney, 2002.

Woodcock, George, and Avacumovic, Ivan, *The Anarchist Prince: A Biographical Study of Peter Kropotkin*, (1950), New York, 1970.

Bibliography

Worsley, Peter, *Knowledges, Culture, Counterculture, Subculture*, New York, 1997.

Worsnop, Thomas, *The Prehistoric Arts, Manufactures, Works, Weapons, etc. of the Aborigines of Australia*, Adelaide 1897.

Wright, Alexis, *Grog War*, Broome, WA, 1997.

Index

Index

blowholes, 149
boab trees, *87*, 88, 95–6
Boyle, Helen, 106
Brazil, 211, 226
Britain: nuclear tests, 157–60, 222, 223, 224–5
Brooks (dingo hunter), 122, 220
Broome, 98–100, 101
Brown, Alfred *see* Radcliffe-Brown
Buludja, 60–2, 221

Calyute, 140
camels, 145
Capricornia (Herbert), 74–7, 79–81, 220
Carrolup Native Settlement, 134–6, 221, 222
cattle farming, 84–6, 89
caves, 149
ceremonies, Aboriginal, 40–2, *41*, 47, 49, 50–3, 119
Chatwin, Bruce, 183, 225
children
  Aboriginal upbringing, 67–70
  half-caste, 62–3, 65–6, 71–2, 74–7, 78, 100–1, 123–6, 130–6, 219
  infanticide, 61–2
  lost black, 72–4
  lost white, 70–2
Christison, Robert, 120–1
circumcision, 153
citizenship: Aboriginal rights to Australian, 179, 180–1, 221, 223
civil rights, Aboriginal, 85, 179–81, 221, 222, 223
compensation, and Aborigines, 208–13, 222
compounds, Aboriginal
  adults, 77–9, 189–99, 219
  children, 78, 123–6, 130–4
Confederation of Indigenous Nationalities of Ecuador, 204, 226
Coniston massacre (1928), 122, 220
Connor, Michael, 206–7
Continental Indigenous International Convention, 204, 226
contrition, 18–19
Coober Pedy, 20–1, 219
Cook, Dr Cecil, 78–9
Cook, James, 215
Cossack, 104
Council for Aboriginal Rights, 85
crime
  imprisonment rates, 106
  punishment of Aboriginal, 34, 122
culture, Aboriginal, 39
  ceremonies, 40–2, *41*, 47, 49, 50–3, 119
  mission attempts to break down, 155

novelists, 136–8
  sand stories, 183–5, *184*
  songs, 167–70, 182–3, 195, 196, 220, 224
  see also art, Aboriginal
Curtin, 96–8, 226, 227

Daly, Mick, 179
Dargie, William: paintings by, *178*
Darwin, 83
  Kahlin Compound, 77–9, 219, 220, 221
Darwin, Charles, 36, 46, 216
Dead, Islands of the, 108–10, 112–16, 130, 216, 218, 219
death: Aboriginal beliefs, 115
Derby, 95–6
deserts
  effects on humans, 24–6, *25*
  flora and fauna survival strategies, 22–3
  see also individual deserts by name
dictation tests, 16–17
disease, 8, 110
  sexually transmitted, 109–10, 112, 114–15, 218, 219
dolphins, 118
Dorré Island, 108–10, 112–16, 130, 216, 218, 219
Dreamings exhibition (1988–90), 193
Durkheim, Émile, 48–50, 52–3, 111, 216, 218
duststorms, 149

education, Aboriginal, 134–6, 154, 219, 220, 221
Edward VIII, 153
Elsey, 59–63
employment conditions, Aboriginal
  meat industry, 84–6
  pearl fishing, 98–100
Emu, 157, 158, 222
emus, 145
Engels, Friedrich, 65, 111, 216
Ernabella, 163
Errington, Shelly, 187
espionage, electronic, 43
eucalyptus trees, 6
evolution, theory of, 36, 46–8
Eylmann, Erhard, 171
Eyre, Edward John, 4–5, 7–10, 216

Faeroe Islands, 26
families, Aboriginal
  family life, 66–70
  kinship, 112–16, 118–20, 123–4, 126–9, 221
Favenc, Ernest, 29–32, 217
Fitzroy Crossing, 89–90

Index

Martin, Catherine, 69–70, 72–4, 216, 219
Marx, Karl, 65
meat industry, 84–6, 89
medical care: Aborigines, 109–10, 112, 114–15, 131, 218, 219
Metropolitan Museum of Art, New York, 224
Meunier, Paul Gaston *see* Réja, Marcel
migrations, Aboriginal, 166–7, 182
Millicent (Little Milli), 123–6, 221, 223, 226
mining
    gold, 57, 144
    opals, 20
missile tests, 15–16, 221
missionaries, 154–8, 165, 220, 222
Mjöberg, Eric, 90–5, *91*, 218
Mogumber Mission/Farm, 133
Monkey Mia, 118
Moore River Native Settlement, 130–4, 219, 220, 222, 226, 227
Moorundie, 4–10, 216
    massacre (1841), 7–9, 216
Morgan, Lewis Henry, 64–5, 111, 216
Morris, Henry C., 37, 217
Mowaljarlai, David: drawings by, *27*
Mudrooroo *see* Johnson, Colin
Mulvaney, D. J., 35
Munn, Nancy D., 182–4, 222, 224
Murray River Valley, 138–41, 216
Museum of Modern Art, New York, 186–7, 220, 221, 222
Museum of Primitive Art, New York, 187, 222
myths, 23–4, 166–7, 197, 219

Namagu, Gladys, 179
Namatjira, Albert, 177–9, *178*, 180–1, 220, 222–3
Namibia, 211
Napangardi, Dorothy, *198*
National Art Gallery, Canberra, 193
Native Americans, 64, 211, 221, 225
natural selection, 36, 46–8
Nelson, Edward, 200, 217
Neville, Octavius, 130–3
Ngaiawong people, 7–9
Norseman, 147
North Australian Workers Union, 85
Norway: resentment of Sweden, 11–12
novelists, Aboriginal, 136–8, 223
nuclear test sites, 157–60, 222, 223–4, 224–5
Nullarbor, 148–51, 215
Nundroo Roadhouse, 149
Nyngar people, 140–1

Oedipus complex, 50–2, 218
Ooldea, 151–60, 218, 219, 220, 221, 222
opals, 20, 215, 219

Papunya, 163, 181, 188–96, 224
Pat, John, 104–6, 225, 226
pearl fishing, 98–100
Peel, Thomas, 138–9, 140
Picasso, Pablo, 200–1
Pierce, Peter, 70–2, 74
Pilkington, Doris, 133, 226
Pinjarra, 139–41
    massacre (1834), 140–1, 216
Pitt-Rivers, George H. L.-F., 37
police: treatment of Aborigines
    Alice Springs, 32–5, 216–17
    Forrest River reserve, 121–2, 219–20
    Roebourne, 104–6, 225, 226
    Sandstone, 112
    STD round-ups, 109–10, 112, 133
population, Australian
    Aborigines as percentage, 44
    density, 16
Port Augusta, 14
Port Hedland, 103–4
    rock art, *105*
Possum, Clifford, 193, 225
Preston, Margaret, 176–7, 219
prisons, 95–6, 104
    imprisonment rates, 106
publishers, Aboriginal, 102

Rabbit-Proof Fence (film), 133, 227
Radcliffe-Brown, Alfred, 111–16, 118–20, 218, 219
radio, Aboriginal, 169
railways, 153, 218, 219
rape, 32–4, 125
reciprocity, 126–9
refugees, 17–18, 96–8, 104, 222, 226, 227
Réja, Marcel (Paul Gaston Meunier), 185–6, 218
religion
    Aboriginal, 47, 49–50, 119
    Aborigines' relationship to land, 163–70, 182, 197
    missionaries, 154–8, 165, 220, 222
Richards, I. A., 207
Rivers, William, 111, 127
rock art, *105*, 170–1, *172*, 216
Roebourne, 104–6, 225
Rover Thomas, 199, 226
Rowley, C. D., 202–3, 224

Sahara, 43
salt industry, 103

247